Political Polarization in American Politics

Political Polarization in American Politics

Edited by
Daniel J. Hopkins and John Sides

Bloomsbury Academic
An imprint of Bloomsbury Publishing Inc

B L O O M S B U R Y
NEW YORK · LONDON · NEW DELHI · SYDNEY

Bloomsbury Academic

An imprint of Bloomsbury Publishing Inc

1385 Broadway	50 Bedford Square
New York	London
NY 10018	WC1B 3DP
USA	UK

www.bloomsbury.com

BLOOMSBURY and the Diana logo are trademarks of Bloomsbury Publishing Plc

First published 2015

Library of Congress Cataloging-in-Publication Data
A catalog record for this book is available from the Library of Congress.

ISBN: PB: 978-1-5013-0627-3
ePDF: 978-1-5013-0629-7
ePub: 978-1-5013-0628-0

Typeset by Deanta Global Publishing Services, Chennai, India
Printed and bound in the United States of America

Contents

Why are we polarized?

CONTENTS

Preface

For several months beginning in late 2012, *The Monkey Cage*—a blog about politics and political science that is part of the *Washington Post*—began a series of posts about polarization. We solicited contributions from a number of scholars, and many more scholars volunteered to offer their perspectives as well.

The result is a collection of pieces from leading experts on polarization that covers nearly every facet of the issue: how American politics became more polarized over time, how much that trend is manifest in different places (Congress, state legislatures, activists, and citizens), what factors are driving that trend, and what reforms might mitigate it.

These pieces puncture some of the myths that frequently appear in casual punditry about polarization—such as the notion that it's mostly driven by politicians who simply don't like each other, or that we can blame it primarily on partisan news media. Instead, polarization has deeper structural and historical roots. Indeed, it may even be the norm in American politics. As such, there are no easy solutions—certainly none as easy as having politicians sit down to dinner with each other.

We have compiled these pieces into this volume so that they can be read together, thereby highlighting the conversation among them. We also hope that this volume will provide these pieces a second life beyond *The Monkey Cage* or the Internet more generally. We thank all of the contributors, and we especially thank Bloomsbury Press and Matthew Kopel for their interest in and support of this project.

Daniel J. Hopkins
John Sides

Contributors

Alan I. Abramowitz is the Alben W. Barkley Professor of Political Science at Emory University, USA. He is the author of *The Disappearing Center: Engaged Citizens, Polarization and American Democracy* and *The Polarized Public: Why American Government Is So Dysfunctional*.

Samuel Abrams is associate professor of politics at Sarah Lawrence College, USA. He and Morris Fiorina are the authors of *Culture War: The Myth of a Polarized America* (with Jeremy Pope) and *Disconnect: The Breakdown of Representation in American Politics*.

Kevin Arceneaux is a professor of political science and director of the Behavioral Foundations Lab at Temple University, USA.

David W. Brady is the Bowen H. and Janice Arthur McCoy Professor of Political Science and Leadership Values at Stanford University, USA, and the deputy director of the Hoover Institution.

David Broockman is a political science graduate student at the University of California, Berkeley, USA.

Thomas Carsey is the Pearsall Distinguished Professor of Political Science and the director of the Odum Institute for Research in Social Science at the University of North Carolina at Chapel Hill, USA.

Morris P. Fiorina is the Wendt Family Professor of Political Science at Stanford University, USA, and a senior fellow at the Hoover Institution.

Robert Ford is lecturer in politics at the University of Manchester, UK, and author (with Matthew Goodwin) of *Revolt on the Right: Explaining Support for the Radical Right in Britain*. He is coauthor of the Polling Observatory, a regular blog on British public opinion. His twitter handle is @robfordmancs.

Andrew Gelman is a professor of statistics and political science at Columbia University, USA. His books include *Bayesian Data Analysis, Teaching Statistics: A Bag of Tricks* and *Red State, Blue State, Rich State, Poor State: Why Americans Vote the Way They Do*.

Hahrie Han is an associate professor of political science at Wellesley College, USA, and the author of two forthcoming books: *How Organizations Develop Activists: Civic Associations and Leadership in the 21st Century* and *Groundbreakers: How Obama's 2.2 Million Volunteers Transformed Field Campaigns in America*.

Christopher Hare is a PhD candidate in political science at the University of Georgia, USA.

Daniel J. Hopkins is associate professor in the Department of Government at Georgetown University, USA. He is the author of many articles on American politics, public opinion, immigration, and political methodology. He contributes to *The Monkey Cage* and 538.

Richard Johnston is Canada Research Chair in public opinion, elections, and representation at the University of British Columbia, Canada.

Geoffrey Layman is professor and director of graduate studies in political science at the University of Notre Dame, USA.

Frances E. Lee is a professor in the Government and Politics Department at the University of Maryland, USA.

Matthew Levendusky is associate professor of political science at the University of Pennsylvania, USA. He is the author of *How Partisan Media Polarize America*.

Robert J. Lieber is professor of government and international affairs at Georgetown University, USA. His latest book is *Power and Willpower in the American Future: Why the United States Is Not Destined to Decline.*

Neil Malhotra is associate professor at the Stanford Graduate School of Business, USA.

Seth Masket is a political scientist at the University of Denver, USA. He blogs regularly at *Mischiefs of Faction* and *Pacific Standard* and tweets at @smotus.

Lilliana Mason is a visiting scholar at Rutgers University, USA. In the fall of 2015, she will be an assistant professor of government and politics at the University of Maryland, USA.

Nolan McCarty is the Susan Dod Brown Professor of Politics and Public Affairs at Princeton University, USA. He has written extensively on political polarization, the politics of inequality, and economic and financial policy-making.

Hans Noel is an associate professor of government at Georgetown University, USA. He specializes in political parties, coalitions, and nomination politics. He is the author of *Political Ideologies and Political Parties in America* and a coauthor of *The Party Decides: Presidential Nominations Before and After Reform*.

Richard Pildes is the Sudler Family Professor of Constitutional Law at New York University, USA, and author of *Why the Center Does Not Hold: The Causes of Hyperpolarized Democracy in America*.

Keith T. Poole is the Philip H. Alston Jr. Distinguished Professor in the Department of Political Science at the University of Georgia, USA. He and Christopher Hare, along with Dave Armstrong, Ryan Bakker, Royce Carroll, and Howard Rosenthal, are coauthors of the forthcoming book *Analyzing Spatial Models of Choice and Judgment with R*.

Howard Rosenthal is professor of politics at New York University, USA, and Roger Williams Straus Professor of Social Sciences, Emeritus, at Princeton University, USA.

Robert Y. Shapiro is a professor of political science at Columbia University, USA. His most recent book is *Selling Fear*.

Boris Shor is a visiting professor at Georgetown University, USA.

John Sides is associate professor in the Department of Political Science at George Washington University, USA. He is the coauthor of *The Gamble*, a book about the 2012 campaign, and scholarly articles on campaign strategy and its effects, attitudes toward immigration, and other topics. He contributes to *The Monkey Cage*.

Jeff Stonecash studies the changing electoral bases of American political parties. He is Emeritus Maxwell Professor at Syracuse University, USA.

Sean Theriault is a professor in the Government Department at the University of Texas, USA. He is the author of three books, including most recently *The Gingrich Senators*.

1

What we know and do not know about our polarized politics

Nolan McCarty

Numerous times over the past several years Americans have witnessed how the lack of compromise and effective negotiation are central problems in our political system. The bigger challenge is explaining how this came about, and what can be done about it. To this end, Jane Mansbridge, Harvard political theorist and past president of the American Political Science Association (APSA), and Cathie Jo Martin convened an APSA task force to lay out an intellectual agenda for the study of political negotiation and promote the many insights from political science, psychology, and economics that might help improve negotiations and facilitate compromise.[1]

As part of this project, I was asked to head a subgroup that focused on how rising levels of polarization and

[1] Jane Mansbridge and Cathie Jo Martin, "Task Force on Negotiating Agreement in Politics," *American Political Science Association*, accessed September 22, 2014. http://www.apsanet.org/negotiatingagreement/.

gridlock have impeded negotiation, compromise, and good governance. By design, the polarization subgroup reflected a variety of viewpoints with respect to the nature and effects of polarized politics in the United States. But in the spirit of a task force on negotiation and compromise, I believe that the report reflects a reasonable consensus about what political scientists know (and, more importantly, do not know) about partisan polarization. So the report serves as a useful point of embarkation for a book on polarization.[2]

Here are the main points of agreement, briefly stated. Readers are encouraged to check out the actual report for the details.

- Based on both qualitative and quantitative evidence, the roots of our current polarization go back almost 40 years to the mid-1970s. Indices of polarization based on roll call voting in Congress show that polarization has increased significantly in both chambers of Congress since around 1978 (see Figures 1 and 2). This evidence is primarily important for the explanations of polarization that it rules out. It casts doubt on explanations focused on more contemporary events such as the Clinton impeachment, the 2000 presidential election, the election of Barack Obama or the emergence of the Tea Party. That both chambers have been affected suggests a limited role for explanations based on the institutional differences

[2]Michael Barber and Nolan McCarty, "Task Force on Negotiating Agreement in Politics," *American Political Science Association* (2013): 19–53.

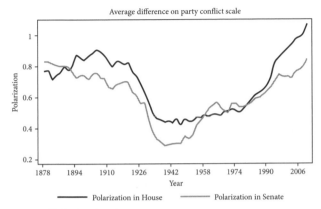

Figure 1 Polarization in congress.

between the House and the Senate. The timing is much more consistent with explanations based on large historical trends such as the post-Civil Rights realignment of southern politics and increased levels of economic and social inequality.

- The evidence points to a major partisan asymmetry in polarization. Despite the widespread belief that both parties have moved to the extremes, the movement of the Republican Party to the right accounts for most of the divergence between the two parties. Since the 1970s, each new cohort of Republican legislators has taken more conservative positions on legislation than the cohorts before them. That is not true of Democratic legislators. Any movement to the left by the Democrats can be accounted for by a decline in

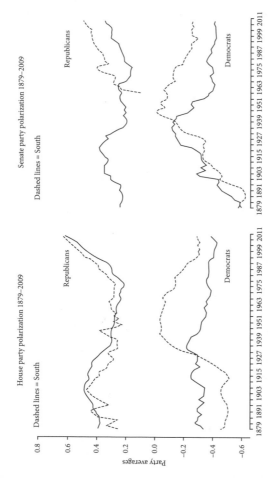

Figure 2 *Average Ideology Score by Party and Region*. The *y*-axis shows the mean position of each party by region. In this plot, the South is defined as AL, AR, FL, GA, KY, LA, MS, NC, OK, SC, TN, TX, and VA. There were no Southern Republican Senators between 1913 and 1960 and only two before that.

white representatives from the South and an increase in African-American and Latino representation.

- The increase in party polarization has also reduced the dimensionality of political conflict. Many issues that were once distinct from the party conflict dimension have been absorbed into it. Congressional voting can be increasingly accounted for by a single dimension that distinguishes the parties. This situation directly contrasts with that of the mid-twentieth century, when the parties divided internally on a variety of issues, especially those related to race and region. While public opinion remains more multidimensional than congressional voting, there is a similar trend among the public.

- While significant disagreement persists as to how much voters have polarized by taking increasingly extreme views, there is a consensus that voters are much better sorted within the party system. Conservative voters are much more likely to identify as Republicans and liberals as Democrats than two generations ago. Moreover, voters' partisanship increasingly predicts their positions on issues. Voters are primarily changing their issue positions to match the partisanship rather than switching to the party that reflects their stances on issues. Since voters seem to be responding to the positions of their party leaders, the causal arrow seems to run from elite polarization to partisan sorting. Whether partisan sorting has an additional feedback effect on elite polarization is less clear.

- Features of our electoral system such as political gerrymandering and partisan primaries are not likely to be important causes of polarization. That the House and Senate have polarized in tandem suggests that partisan districting cannot be a primary cause and researchers have failed to find much of an incremental contribution. Similarly, scholars have not identified any substantial impact of the primary system on polarization. The relationship between our system of private campaign finance and polarization is more complex. While there is little evidence that the origins of greater polarization lie in campaign finance, the growing participation of ideologically oriented donors appears to have exacerbated the problem.

- Polarization in Congress derives from both sincere ideological differences about policy means and ends and strategic behavior to exploit those differences to win elections. The combination of high ideological stakes and intense competition for party control of the national government has all but eliminated the incentives for significant bipartisan cooperation on important national problems. Consequently, polarization has reduced congressional capacity to govern. Congress has been less productive in legislation, more prone to delays in appropriating funds, and increasingly slow in handling executive and judicial appointments. While hard to quantify, there is considerable evidence for a decline in the quality of legislative deliberation and legislation. Of significant concern is the extent to which this reduction in legislative capacity has contributed to a shift in the constitutional balance, as it enhanced opportunities for executive and judicial encroachments on legislative prerogatives.

In this book, various political and social scientists weigh in on different questions related to political polarization, both in government, among American voters, and abroad. These chapters will tackle the puzzle of polarization from various angles.

The first set of chapters examines how we are polarized—including evidence from the US Congress, state legislatures, and voters. The second set of chapters investigates why we are polarizing. Is it due to partisan news media, for example? The third set of chapters looks at polarization in other countries, such as Great Britain and Canada. Finally, the last chapters consider the future trajectory of polarization and whether anything could reduce polarization.

Discussion questions

- What causes of polarization does the author identify and what causes does the author eliminate as explanations?

- Why has polarization reduced the "capacity to govern"?

Further reading

McCarty, Nolan, Keith T. Poole, and Howard Rosenthal (2006), *Polarized America: The Dance of Ideology and Unequal Riches.* Cambridge, MA: The MIT Press.

How are we polarized?

2

Partisan warfare is the problem

Sean Theriault

I have been studying party polarization in Congress for more than a decade. The more I study it, the more I question that it is the root cause of what Americans hate about Congress. Pundits and political scientists alike point to party polarization as the culprit for all sorts of congressional ills. I, too, have contributed to this chorus bemoaning party polarization.[1] But increasingly, I have come to think that our problem today is not just polarization in Congress; it is the related but more serious problem of political warfare.

I think that Evan Bayh (D-Ind.), as he announced his retirement from the Senate, best articulates the conventional wisdom:

> For some time, I've had a growing conviction that Congress is not operating as it should. There is much too much partisanship and not enough progress; too much narrow ideology and not enough practical problem-solving. Even

[1]Sean M. Theriault, *Party Polarization in Congress* (New York: Cambridge University Press, 2008).

at a time of enormous national challenge, the people's business is not getting done … I love working for the people of Indiana. I love helping our citizens make the most of their lives. But I do not love Congress.[2]

It could be that I am splitting hairs, but the more I research polarization, the less I agree that "much too much partisanship" halts "progress" or that "too much narrow ideology" impedes "practical problem-solving."

In more recent work, I explore a second and admittedly related dimension of political competition.[3] Actually, I called it "partisan warfare" in this book, but I think "political warfare" is more accurate, because partisanship is not always the cause. While it, too, may have its roots in party polarization, political warfare is more combative in nature and requires more than what can be revealed by voting patterns on the Senate floor. The warfare dimension taps into the strategies that go beyond defeating your opponents to humiliating them, go beyond questioning your opponents' judgment to questioning their motives, and go beyond fighting the good legislative fight to destroying the institution and the legislative process. Political warfare serves electoral goals, not legislative goals.

---

[2]Lynn Sweet, "Sen. Evan Bayh Won't Run Again: 'Congress is Not Operating as it Should' Transcript," *Chicago Sun-Times*, February 15, 2010. http://www.blogs.suntimes.com/sweet/2010/02/sen_evan_bayh_wont_run_again_c.html.

[3]Sean M. Theriault, *The Gingrich Senators: The Roots of Partisan Warfare in Congress* (Oxford: Oxford University Press, 2013).

This warfare certainly has party polarization at its roots. Polarization may be necessary for warfare, but it is not a sufficient cause of it. Parties that are divided over policy can have a serious and honest debate, which can even become heated. In the first half of the famous idiom, the opposing sides can "agree to disagree." Quite apart from the serious policy disagreement, though, the debate between the opposing sides can degenerate into a shouting match in which the policy prescriptions are lost in a fight over legislative games and in which the combatants question the motives, integrity, and patriotism of their opponents. Under such a situation, the second half of the idiom—"without being disagreeable"—is never realized.

This partisan warfare dimension is harder to quantify, though it most certainly exists. What I call "warfare" is what Frances Lee characterized as "beyond ideology" in her book of the same name.[4] Lee argues that only so much of the divide between the parties can be understood as a difference in ideology. The rest of the divide—by some accounts, the lion's share of the divide—is motivated by some other goal. I argue that it is this portion of the divide, the divide beyond ideology, which causes the angst of participants and observers of today's Senate.

More often than not, congressional scholars and political pundits have opted to merge these two dimensions for a couple of reasons. First, there is no doubt that they are related. Party polarization and political warfare are sufficiently similar that

[4]Frances E. Lee, *Beyond Ideology: Politics, Principles, and Partisanship in the U.S. Senate* (Chicago: University of Chicago Press, 2009).

many treat them as synonyms. Second, the second dimension of political warfare, especially in comparison to the first, is much harder to isolate, operationalize, and analyze. Nonetheless, real analytic leverage can be brought to our understanding of how the current Senate operates and how it is evaluated if these dimensions are pulled apart.

Perhaps my home state of Texas unnecessarily reinforces the distinction I want to make between these two dimensions. Little separates my two senators' voting records—of the 279 votes that senators took in 2013, Ted Cruz and John Cornyn disagreed less than 9 percent of the time (the largest category of their disagreement, incidentally, was on confirmation votes). In terms of ideology, they are both very conservative. Cruz, to no one's surprise, is the most conservative.[5] Cornyn is the 13th most conservative, which is actually further down the list than he was in 2012, when he ranked second.[6] Cornyn's voting record is more conservative than conservative stalwarts Tom Coburn and Richard Shelby. Marco Rubio and Ted Cruz disagreed on twice as many votes as John Cornyn and Ted Cruz.

The difference between my senators is that when John Cornyn shows up for a meeting with fellow senators, he

---

[5]Simon Jackman, "113th U.S. Senate: Ideal Points & 95% Credible Intervals," Stanford University, last modified September 19, 2014, accessed September 22, 2014. http://www.jackman.stanford.edu/ideal/currentSenate/x1.pdf.

[6]Todd J. Gillman, "Ranked 2d Most Conservative, Sen. John Cornyn Pushes Back on Ted Cruz-as-Guidestar Narrative," *The Dallas Morning News*, February 20, 2013. http://www.trailblazersblog.dallasnews.com/2013/02/ranked-2d-most-conservative-sen-john-cornyn-pushes-back-on-ted-cruz-as-guidestar-narrative.html/.

brings a pad of paper and pencil and tries to figure out how to solve problems. Ted Cruz, on the other hand, brings a battle plan.

The trick for me, and all those interested in party polarization, is coming up with systematic, repeated behaviors that differentiate ideological legislators from political warriors. The former make legitimate contributions to political discourse in the Congress; the latter do not, and need to be called out for the havoc they wreak on our political system. The Senate has in the past and can continue in the future to accommodate senators with serious disagreements. Too many warriors in the Senate, unfortunately, will only perpetuate the dysfunction and low congressional approval we have seen in the last couple of years.

Discussion questions

- Why does the author believe polarization and partisan warfare should be considered as separate terms?
- If you were trying to measure these terms through the words or behavior of members of Congress, how would you distinguish between them?

Further reading

Theriault, Sean M. (2013), *The Gingrich Senators*. Oxford: Oxford University Press.

3

How US state legislatures are polarized and getting more polarized

Boris Shor

America's state legislatures are polarized—just like Congress—between liberals and conservatives, Democrats and Republicans (see Chapter 1). But just how polarized are they? We have not been able to tell in the past, because we have not been able to determine just how liberal or conservative state legislators are in all fifty states. One major reason why each state is rather unique. Massachusetts Republicans are not the same as Texas Republicans; the same is true for each state's Democrats. Nor do they vote on the same things. These differences mean that measuring ideology—and levels of polarization—is much more difficult for state legislatures than for Congress.

Nolan McCarty and I have come up with a method for overcoming this problem.[1] We have released the resulting

---

[1] "Measurement Papers," *Measuring America Legislatures*, accessed September 22, 2014. http://www.americanlegislatures.com/papers/.

data set for free to the scholarly community and public.[2] This chapter uses those data as well as even more recent data that are currently being cleaned and prepared for public release. Thus, we can analyze polarization through 2013 in most states.

Figure 3 shows the legislative polarization in each state, averaging across all the years of our data (approximately 1996–2013) and across both legislative chambers. Polarization is defined as the average ideological distance between the median Democrat and Republican in the state legislature. Larger numbers indicate more division. The dashed line is the level of congressional polarization, included as a comparison ("US").

About half of the states are even more polarized than Congress—which is saying a lot. At the same time, some states—like Louisiana, Delaware, and Rhode Island—have relatively less polarized state legislatures. In Louisiana, both parties are fairly conservative, and in Delaware and Rhode Island, they are both fairly liberal.

One state that stands out is California. It is incredibly polarized. (And its most recent primary and redistricting reforms look unlikely to reduce polarization.)[3] Unlike Congress, however, Democrats both dominate the state so thoroughly and no longer need to attain supermajorities to

---

[2]"Aggregate Data," *Measuring America Legislatures*, accessed September 22, 2014. http://www.americanlegislatures.com/papers/.

[3]Thad Kousser, Justin Phillips, and Boris Shor, "Reform and Representation: Assessing California's Top-Two Primary and Redistricting Commission," *Social Science Research Network*, 2013.

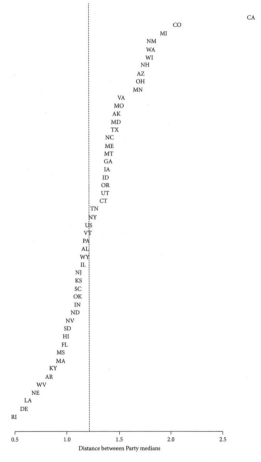

Figure 3 Average legislative polarization.

pass budgets, so this polarization is not as much of an obstacle to actual lawmaking in the California state legislature.

Another state that stands out is Wisconsin—the site of massive protests in 2011, a recall campaign against sitting governor Scott Walker, and even a physical fight between Republican and Democratic justices on its state Supreme Court.[4] It is perhaps no surprise that Wisconsin too is highly polarized.

Not only are states polarized, that polarization has increased over time.[5] Figure 4 breaks down the trends in the ideology of Democrats and Republicans (measured by party medians) over time and across all fifty states. By convention, more positive scores represent more conservative preferences, and more negative scores represent liberal preferences. (One side-note: a data error exists in Washington State around the year 2000 and is being fixed.)

Most states have polarized over the past 20 years or so, but some more than others. Arizona, California, and Colorado are polarizing very fast. Nebraska—a state without formal

[4]"2011 Wisconsin Protests," *Wikipedia*, accessed September 22, 2014. http://www.en.wikipedia.org/wiki/2011_Wisconsin_protests; "Wisconsin Gubernatorial Recall Election," *Wikipedia*, accessed September 22, 2014. http://www.en.wikipedia.org/wiki/Wisconsin_gubernatorial_recall_election; See Chapter 3.
[5]"Polarization Trends in American State Legislatures by Chamber," *Measuring American Legislatures*, July 26, 2013. http://www.americanlegislatures.com/2013/07/26/polarization-trends-in-american-state-legislatures-by-chamber/.

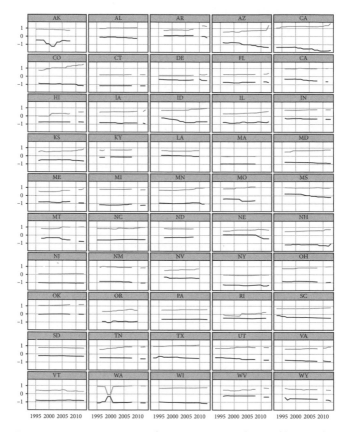

Figure 4 Average party medians over time. The gray line is the Republican party median and the black line is the Democratic party median.

political parties in its legislature—is polarizing very quickly too, though from a relatively low base.[6]

Moreover, we are seeing asymmetric polarization, just as Chapter 1 detailed at the federal level. Republicans have been getting more extreme faster than Democrats in more state legislative chambers, but this is by no means universally true across all states.[7]

All in all, the picture we see in state legislatures is similar in many respects to Congress, but different in key points. The parties are pretty far apart on average, but that difference varies across the states. The parties are increasingly polarizing over time, but that too varies across state. Finally, we see cases of symmetric and asymmetric polarization. These new data on polarization at the state level—and the uneven pace of polarization across states—should help pundits and scholars figure out what is driving polarization in our statehouses.

Discussion questions

- What is the relationship between polarization at the federal and state level?

- How are the authors measuring polarization?

[6]Seth E. Masket and Boris Short, "Polarization Without Parties: The Rise of Legislative Partisanship in Nebraska's Unicameral Legislature," *Social Science Research Network*, 2011.
[7]"Asymmetric Polarization in the State Legislatures? Yes and No," *Measuring American Legislatures*, July 29, 2013. http://www.americanlegislatures.com/2013/07/29/partisan-polarization-in-state-legislatures/; See Chapter 1.

Further reading

Shor, Boris and Nolan McCarty (2011), "The Ideological Mapping of American Legislatures," *American Political Science Review* 105(3): 530–51.

4

Our politics is polarized on more issues than ever before

Thomas Carsey and Geoffrey Layman

The Democratic and Republican parties are as far apart on issues of public policy as they have been in at least a half-century (see Chapter 1). The clear growth in polarization between the parties' elected officials, activists, and coalitions in the mass electorate is well recognized and has been widely touted by political observers, leaders, and scholars (see the reviews by Juliana Horowitz and us, as well as Marc Hetherington, of the vast academic literature on polarization).[1] However, we believe that much of the public discussion of party polarization misses two important points. First, far from being something new, party polarization has been the natural state of American politics throughout our

[1]Geoffrey C. Layman, Thomas M. Carsey, and Juliana M. Horowitz, "Party Polarization in American Politics: Characteristics, Causes, and Consequences," *Annual Review of Political Science* 9 (2006): 83–110; Marc J. Hetherington, "Putting Polarization in Perspective," *British Journal of Political Science* 39, 2 (2009): 413–48.

history. Second, contemporary party polarization may well be different, characterized by what we call "conflict extension."

Since they first formed at the end of the eighteenth century, the major American parties have nearly always been polarized over some set of policy issues.[2] The most famous and tragic example is, of course, slavery. But battles over issues like the relative power of the national and state governments (embodied in the early debates about a national bank), the Gold Standard, the New Deal, and civil rights resulted in deep divisions between the nation's political parties. Party polarization is not new. In fact, a primary function of political parties is to clearly organize political conflict, making some clear policy separation between the parties virtually inevitable.[3]

However, the conventional wisdom in political science says that for most of our history such party polarization applied to only one general policy area at a time. New divisions only emerged when they successfully pushed the old division that had dominated political conflict to the side. This process, called conflict displacement, meant that parties were not locked into polarized positions on every major issue facing the country.[4] The parties might be polarized on one major issue but still able to cooperate on various others.

[2]James L. Sundquist, *Dynamics of the Party System: Alignment and Realignment of Political Parties in the United States* (Washington: Brookings Institution Press, 1983).
[3]Sundquist, *Dynamics of the Party System*, 1983.
[4]Elmer E. Schattschneider, *The Semi-Sovereign People: A Realist's View of Democracy in America* (Boston: Cengage Learning, 1975); Sundquist, *Dynamics of the Party System*, 1983.

Our research suggests that the process of conflict displacement has itself been replaced by what we call conflict extension.[5] Thus, while party polarization is not new, growing polarization across multiple issue dimensions may well be new. Figure 5 illustrates what we mean with data from the American National Election Studies (ANES) series of national opinion surveys. The graph shows the degree of polarization between citizens who identify themselves as Democrats and Republicans on four different issues that were asked about consistently from 1972 through 2012.

Two questions—whether it is government's responsibility to ensure that everyone has a job and a good standard of living and whether government should provide health insurance for all citizens—harken to the political divisions over social welfare that emerged with the New Deal. A question about the government's responsibility to help improve the social and economic position of African-Americans taps into divisions on civil rights that emerged in the 1960s. A question about the legality of abortion represents the cultural and moral issues that have separated the parties since the 1980s. All issues have been scaled to range from zero for the most liberal position to one for the most conservative position, and the figure shows the difference in party means.

The most important feature is the clear trend toward greater polarization on all four issues. Had conflict displacement occurred, as it did in prior epochs, the increase

[5]Geoffrey C. Layman and Thomas M. Carsey, "Party Polarization and 'Conflict Extension' in the American Electorate," *American Journal of Political Science* 46, 4 (2002): 786–802.

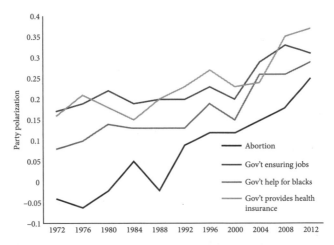

Figure 5 Party polarization on four issues, 1972–2012.
Source: 1972–2012 American National Election Studies.

in polarization on newer issues like abortion would have coincided with less polarization on older issues such as race and social welfare. Instead, polarization on these older issues has actually increased.

Moreover, the same conflict extension is evident among members of Congress and the activists represented at the parties' national conventions. Figure 6 is adapted from one of our recent academic publications and shows levels of party polarization on social welfare, racial, and cultural issues (standardized to a mean of 50 and a standard deviation of 25) for the parties in Congress (based on congressional roll call votes), party activists (based on surveys of national

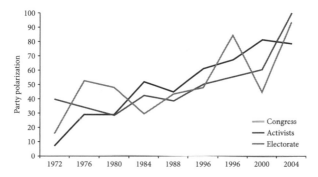

Figure 6 Party polarization on social welfare issues.

Note: Levels of party polarization have been standardized to a mean of 50 and a standard deviation of 25.

Source: 1972–2004 Convention Delegate Studies, American National Election Studies, and Congressional Roll Call Votes.

party convention delegates), and the party identifiers in the electorate (based on ANES data).[6]

The same is true for racial issues and cultural issues, as Figures 7 and 8 demonstrate.

The data are clear: across all three major domestic issue areas—social welfare, race, and culture—there has been a steady increase in the gap between Democratic and

[6]Geoffrey C. Layman, Thomas M. Carsey, John C. Green, Richard Herrera, and Rosalyn Cooperman, "Activists and Conflict Extension in American Party Politics," *American Political Science Review* 104, 2 (2010): 324–46; "Convention Delegate Study Series," *Interuniversity Consortium for Political and Social Research*, accessed September 22, 2014. http://www.icpsr.umich.edu/icpsrweb/ICPSR/series/00116.

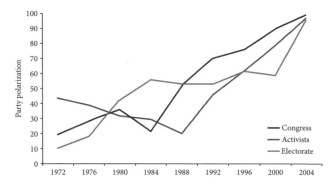

Figure 7 Party polarization on racial issues.

Note: Levels of party polarization have been standardized to a mean of 50 and a standard deviation of 25.

Source: 1972–2004 Convention Delegate Studies, American National Election Studies, and Congressional Roll Call Votes.

Republican citizens, elected officials, and activists. In short, we have witnessed conflict extension.

These data raise an obvious question: who leads the process of conflict extension and who follows? No doubt trends among citizens, elected officials, and party activists all influence each other. However, our research suggests that party activists have been the key catalyst.[7]

Activists are more likely than elected officials and ordinary citizens to champion ideologically extreme positions on new issues and bring them into the party system, and changes

[7]Layman et al., "Activists and Conflict Extension in American Party Politics," 324–46.

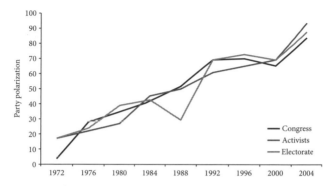

Figure 8 Party polarization on cultural issues.

Note: Levels of party polarization have been standardized to a mean of 50 and a standard deviation of 25.

Source: 1972–2004 Convention Delegate Studies, American National Election Studies, and Congressional Roll Call Votes.

in our party system have made it easier for activist groups to enter party politics. Since the 1960s, the Democratic and Republican parties have steadily lowered barriers to participation in party politics. Nomination processes have moved out of the hands of party bosses and into the hands of primary and caucus participants. Activist groups and candidates themselves are increasingly able to finance their own campaigns without the help of parties. In several instances, the parties have actively recruited newly politicized groups into the party rank-and-file.

Thus, part of the reason why party polarization in earlier periods may have been limited to one issue area at a time is that party leaders made it harder for activists and insurgents to enter the party system. This has changed, and polarized groups of activists have helped to polarize the parties on multiple policy agendas.

Conflict extension has evolved to such a degree that insurgent groups who in the past might press a single-issue agenda are now likely to advance more strident positions across multiple issues. For example, recent research by David Campbell and Robert Putnam shows that while Tea Party activists tend to emphasize economic and small-government conservatism, they are equally conservative on cultural issues. Similarly, activists from groups like Occupy Wall Street, religious seculars, and members of the lesbian, gay, bisexual, and transgender (LGBT) community who are typically associated with liberalism on a single-issue agenda tend to hold strongly liberal views across all issue agendas.[8]

Where does this leave us? Current discussions of party polarization must recognize that polarization in general is not new. The two major parties almost always have disagreed deeply about some policy issues. However, what may be different is the emergence of party polarization across all major dimensions of domestic political debate. That political polarization seems, to most people, to be worse now than in prior eras may be due partly to this conflict extension. Where parties in earlier periods may have found many areas of agreement even as they fought bitterly over some issues, parties today disagree on virtually everything.

[8]David E. Campbell and Robert D. Putnam, "Crashing the Tea Party," *The New York Times*, last modified August 16, 2011, accessed September 22, 2014. http://www.nytimes.com/2011/08/17/opinion/crashing-the-tea-party.html?_r=2&.

Discussion questions

- What is the difference between conflict extension and conflict displacement?

- Why is conflict extension relevant to discussions of polarization?

- What theory do the authors use to explain the increased polarization through conflict extension? Do you find it convincing?

Further reading

Layman, Geoffrey C., Thomas M. Carsey, John C. Green, Richard Herrera, and Rosalyn Cooperman (2010), "Activists and Conflict Extension in American Party Politics," *American Political Science Review* 104(2): 324–46.

5

How politically moderate are Americans? Less than it seems

Christopher Hare and Keith T. Poole

To the extent that any topic in the social sciences can be considered settled, the polarization of American political elites almost certainly qualifies. In Congress, the distance between the parties' ideological positions—whether measured using roll call voting records or campaign contributions—has continued to rise at a record-setting pace since the 1970s.[1] The ideological center in Congress, the driving force behind major policy reforms as recently as the 1980s, has hollowed out.

A much more contested question concerns the degree to which the mass electorate can also be described as polarized. Political scientist Morris Fiorina and his colleagues (especially with their book *Culture War? The Myth of a*

---

[1] "The Polarization of the Congressional Parties," *Vote View*, January 19, 2014. http://www.voteview.com/political_polarization.asp; John Sides, "New Data on Ideology and Money in Politics," *The Monkey Cage*, July 25, 2013. http://www.themonkeycage.org/2013/07/25/new-data-on-ideology-and-money-in-politics/.

Polarized America) have been the leading advocates for the position that ordinary Americans remain predominantly centrist and are alienated by elite polarization (see Chapter 6).[2] While it is true that most Americans consider themselves to be near the center of the ideological spectrum (either moderates or "slightly" liberal or conservative using the standard seven-point liberal-conservative scale), there are two reasons to expect that many of these moderates are illusory.[3] In truth, the American electorate is more polarized ideologically than it might seem at first glance. And that is especially true for those voters who are more knowledgeable about politics.

First, moderates possess lower levels of political information and are less likely to be politically engaged than those who are closer to one of the ideological poles. As a result, centrists are underrepresented in the electorate. Emory University political scientist Alan Abramowitz has extensively detailed this phenomenon in his book *The Disappearing Center*.[4]

Second, the term "moderate" is a favorable term in politics, one that connotes pragmatism and reasonableness, as opposed to epithets like ideologue, radical, or extremist.

[2]Morris P. Fiorina, Samuel J. Abrams, and Jeremy C. Pope, *Culture War? The Myth of a Polarized America* (Upper Saddle River: Pearson, 2010). See Chapter 6.
[3]"The ANES Guide to Public Opinion and Electoral Behavior," *American National Election Studies*, accessed September 22, 2014. http://www.electionstudies.org/nesguide/toptable/tab3_1.htm.
[4]Alan I. Abramowitz, *The Disappearing Center: Engaged Citizens, Polarization, and American Democracy* (New Haven: Yale University Press, 2011).

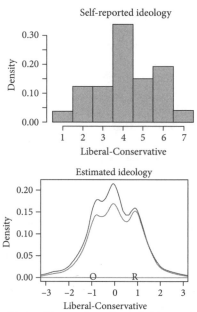

Figure 9 The distribution of self-report and estimated ideology. "O" indicates the location of Obama and "R" indicates the location of Romney.
Data source: 2012 American National Election Study.

Accordingly, many individuals describe themselves and their preferred candidate and party as "moderate." Indeed, in the 2012 American National Election Study (the data we use here), 31 percent of Obama voters who placed both themselves and Obama on the liberal-conservative scale rated both themselves and Obama as "moderate" or "slightly liberal," while 21 percent of Romney voters rated both themselves and Romney as "moderate" or "slightly conservative." Of course, if these respondents view themselves as sharing the ideological views of the Democratic or Republican parties, they are probably not really centrists. This is a common problem in survey research known as "differential item functioning," and it occurs any time that respondents interpret scales differently.

We use the Aldrich-McKelvey scaling procedure to uncover both types of moderates: the politically uninformed/ unengaged and the "moderates-in-name-only."[5] Put differently, we use respondents' placements of common objects (e.g., the Republican and Democratic parties) to estimate how they distort the space and correct for bias in their self-placements. For example, someone who rated herself and Obama as "moderate" and placed Romney at the right-most, "extremely conservative" category would be moved to the left.

The scaling procedure also essentially "sorts" respondents by their level of political information. For example, if they place Romney and the Republican Party to the left of Obama and the Democratic Party, they have a very low level of political information. Conversely, respondents who can correctly place the objects are more likely to be politically informed and participate in the political arena.

---

[5]"Bayesian Aldrich-McKelvey Scaling," *Vote View*, accessed September 22, 2014. http://www.voteview.com/BAM.asp.

The top panel of Figure 9 shows respondents' self-placements on the liberal-conservative scale in the left panel, and we see a familiar bell curve pattern where most respondents place themselves in the middle and only a small proportion consider themselves to be "extremely liberal" or "extremely conservative." This paints a clear picture of a centrist electorate.

The bottom panel shows the distribution of respondent ideal points estimated by Bayesian Aldrich-McKelvey scaling, which corrects for bias in respondents' self-placements. The distribution of all respondents is shown in black, while the gray line shows only respondents who correctly place the liberal stimuli to the left of the conservative stimuli (in technical terms, have positive weights in the scaling). Both distributions exhibit greater polarization than the raw self-placements. There is still a peak at the center, but there are also modes around the estimated locations of Obama and Romney (the black "O" and the gray "R" tokens). Many moderates also disappear when we look at only respondents who place the parties appropriately, and the heights of the three modes are nearly equal in this distribution.

Another way to measure polarization from the two sets of ideology scores (the raw self-placements and the adjusted ideal points) is to calculate the overlap between partisan groups and Obama/Romney voters indicated by each set of scores. The more Obama and Romney voters overlap, the lower the level of polarization. Political scientists Matt Levendusky (University of Pennsylvania) and Jeremy Pope (BYU) have pioneered this approach as an alternative measure

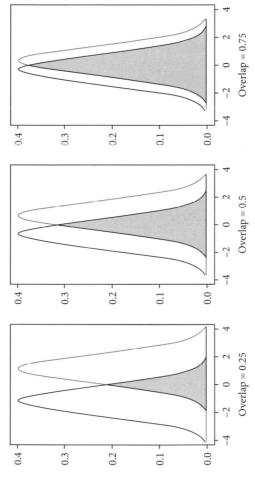

Figure 10 Examples of different overlap coefficients.

of polarization between two opinion distributions.[6] The overlap coefficient ranges between 0 and 1, with higher values indicating greater overlap and lower polarization. Figure 10 shows some examples of what the overlap coefficients look like in three different cases.

We calculate the overlap between Obama and Romney voters and between Democrats and Republicans (including leaners) on the liberal-conservative dimension using each of the two measures: the raw self-placements and the DIF-corrected ideal point estimates. As we might expect, the overlap between both groups is smaller—and thus polarization is greater—using the corrected estimates of ideology as compared to respondents' own self-placements on the liberal-conservative scale. The differences are statistically significant (see Figure 11) and substantial in magnitude: a 38 percent drop (from 0.45 to 0.28) in the overlap between Democrats and Republicans and a 46 percent drop (from 0.48 to 0.26) in the overlap between Obama and Romney voters when moving from raw self-placements to the BAM ideal point estimates. Once we account for differences in how Americans define "liberals," "moderates," and "conservatives," we get a picture of a more polarized electorate than if we rely on raw self-placement data.

[6]"Matthew Levendusky," *University of Pennsylvania*, accessed September 23, 2014. http://www.sas.upenn.edu/polisci/people/standing-faculty/matthew-levendusky; Matthew S. Levendusky and Jeremy C. Pope, "Red States vs. Blue States: Going Beyond the Mean," *Public Opinion Quarterly* 75, 2 (2011): 227–48.

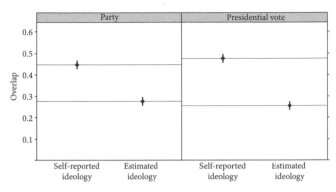

Figure 11 Overlap coefficients with 95 percent confidence intervals.

These results are a classic instance of "a glass half full vs. a glass half empty." Compared to members of the House and Senate, the public is clearly more moderate. The overlap for the House and Senate is zero. There are still moderates in American politics, but they are in the electorate and not in Congress. Still, we cannot characterize the American public as overwhelmingly centrist—doing so is more an artifact of survey responses than an apt description of Americans' ideology.

Discussion question

- Why do the authors need a different measure of "moderate" than simply asking people how they identify?

Further reading

Hare, Christopher, David A. Armstrong II, Ryan Bakker, Royce Carroll, and Keith T. Poole (2015), "Using Bayesian Aldrich-McKelvey Scaling to Study Citizens' Ideological Preferences and Perceptions." *American Journal of Political Science* (forthcoming).

6

Americans are not polarized, just better sorted

Morris P. Fiorina and Samuel Abrams

While much research demonstrates that the political class in the United States has become increasingly polarized, the common claim that the larger electorate also has become more polarized has little basis. Rather, the continuing accumulation of data strongly supports the conclusion that what has occurred in the United States is the sorting of partisan subgroups within the larger population (first identified by Alan Abramowitz and Kyle Saunders).[1]

In the aggregate, today's electorate looks surprisingly similar to that of the 1970s. Following the difficulties experienced by the Democrats between 1964 and 1972, partisanship has since fluctuated within a narrow band, as Figure 12 shows. Self-identified ideology has moved within a similarly narrow band (see Figure 13). Where surveys permit the tracking of individual issues over time, the opinion distributions continue to maintain a centrist shape, and the

[1]Alan I. Abramowitz and Kyle L. Saunders, "Ideological Realignment in the U.S. Electorate," *The Journal of Politics* 60, 3 (1998): 634–52.

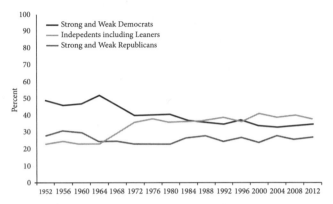

Figure 12   Little change in partisanship since the 1970s.
Source: American National Election Study.

departures tend to show leftward (toward more government services vs. lower taxes) or rightward (toward less role for government in health care and especially aid to minorities) shifts rather than a symmetric shift toward both poles.[2] By no means has the political center vanished.

What has changed is how partisans are distributed in terms of their ideology and issue opinions. Self-identified Democrats have become more homogeneously liberal and self-identified Republicans more homogeneously conservative. And the differences between the two partisan groups on issues have increased, although not nearly as much as those among party elites. For example, ordinary Democrats

[2]"The ANES Guide to Public Opinion and Electoral Behavior," American National Election Studies, accessed September 23, 2014. http://www. electionstudies.org/nesguide/nesguide.htm.

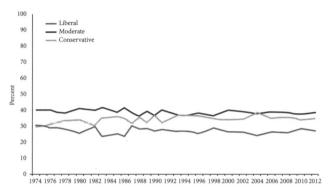

Figure 13   Little change in voter ideology since the 1970s.
Source: General Social Survey.

and Republicans were indistinguishable on abortion until the 1990s and then began to differ (as Figure 14 illustrates), but even in 2012, American National Election Study data indicate that a quarter of Democrats arguably fall into the pro-life category and a third of Republicans into the pro-choice category.

Of course, none of this is to argue that sorting is unimportant. It is, and sorting contributes to the extreme partisanship we see in Washington and many of our state capitals (see Chapters 1 and 3). Compared to two decades ago Democratic candidates are more likely to be liberals than moderates, let alone conservatives, and Republicans more likely to be conservatives than moderates, let alone liberals. Moreover, Democratic candidates face the same kinds of primary constituencies whether they are running in New York or New Mexico, and the same for Republican

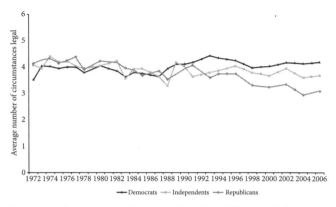

Figure 14 Partisans in the general public differ much less than activists and office-holders on abortion.

Note: Partisans include strong and weak identifiers.

Source: General Social Survey.

officeholders whether running in Minnesota or Missouri. In earlier decades, they were nominated by more heterogeneous supporting constituencies.

The sorting of partisans into parties with clearer identities might result in less satisfaction for *all* categories of voters. According to a 2008 Comparative Study of Electoral Systems (CSES) poll only about 40 percent of Americans felt that the Democratic Party represented their views "reasonably well," about 30 percent believed the Republican Party represented their views "reasonably well," and the other 30 percent believed neither party represented their views. We suspect that these figures would be lower today, but taken at face value, they suggest that an attempt by either party to implement its program would find a less than enthusiastic response among 60–70 percent of the public.

Can the sorting be reversed? Some analysts write as if sorting is an inexorable process, the result of demographic or economic trends that render one electoral coalition inevitably rising or ascendant. But in the argot of political science, electoral coalitions are at least in part endogenous, meaning that they not only shape what politicians do but are shaped by those politicians' actions as well.

Strategic politicians see social and economic changes as opportunities to disrupt old coalitions and construct new ones. Sometimes we can foresee the shape of new coalitions, as when Lyndon Johnson commented that he was giving Republicans the South for a long time to come when he signed the 1964 Civil Rights Act. But in other cases the shape of future coalitions is harder to predict. In 1965 who would have foreseen that environmental protection, abortion, and other cultural issues would begin reshaping electoral coalitions by the late 1970s? While we cannot predict the shape of future electoral coalitions, we believe that the present situation is a not stable equilibrium.

Discussion questions

- What do the authors mean by "better sorted"?
- The authors end the chapter with the assertion that this current situation is not a stable equilibrium. Why do they think that? Do you agree?

Further reading

Fiorina, Morris P. and Samuel J. Abrams (2009), *Disconnect: The Breakdown of Representation in American Politics*. Norman: University of Oklahoma Press.

7

Are politicians and activists reliably "more extreme" than voters? A skeptical perspective

David Broockman

As partisan divisions in Congress have grown, concern has mounted that politicians are pursuing much more extreme policies than nearly all their constituents support.[1] According to a common line of thinking, campaign donors and primary voters are pulling politics to the extremes. Most Americans, the story goes, would prefer their legislators to chart a moderate course.

I question this view. Using a survey designed to measure support for extreme policies, I find that the characterization

---

[1]Morris P. Fiorina and Samuel J. Abrams, *Disconnect: The Breakdown of Representation in American Politics* (Norman: University of Oklahoma Press, 2009); Andrew Gelman, "Left-Right Ideology of Voters, Congressmembers, and Senators," *Statistical Modeling, Causal Inference, and Social Science*, accessed September 23, 2014. http://www.andrewgelman.com/2008/07/22/left-right-ideology-of-voters-congressmembers-and-senators/; Stephen Ansolabehere, Jonathan Rodden, and James M. Snyder Jr., "Purple America," *Journal of Economic Perspectives* 20, 2 (2006): 97–118.

of the public as largely centrist rests on shaky ground.[2] On many issues, much of the public appears to support more extreme policies than legislators do. And while many argue that today's engaged activists support more extreme policies than the broader public, my findings suggest the opposite: The disengaged and infrequent voters who allegedly constitute the moderate middle are actually more likely to endorse extreme policies than politically active voters.

Why might we have missed much extremism in the public generally and among the *less* engaged? The answer is subtle, but has important implications for how we should think about the public's attitudes and politicians' positions. And it might be best explained by pretending you have a crazy uncle.

Suppose your uncle believes that the United States should nationalize the health-care system (a very liberal view) and that gay people should be jailed (a very conservative view). And suppose your uncle is represented in Congress by a moderate Republican who supports civil unions (but opposes gay marriage) and who supports helping the poor purchase health insurance (but opposes Obamacare), two positions just right of center.

Your uncle's views cannot really be described in ideological terms like "center left" or "very conservative." He has some mix of very liberal and very conservative views, many of them extreme. But if we try to compare your uncle's views to

---

[2]David Broockman, "Approaches to Studying Representation," University of California, Berkeley, accessed September 30, 2014. http://www.ocf.berkeley.edu/~broockma/broockman_approaches_to_studying_representation.pdf.

his congressperson's positions in abstract, ideological terms, as academics and journalists often do, some plain facts about your uncle and his legislator both become obscured. Since your uncle supports some liberal policies and some conservative policies, we would call him a "moderate on average." However, his congressperson's conservative votes on both Obamacare and gay marriage mean we might call the legislator conservative. We thus might condemn your uncle's congressperson for being a conservative extremist while celebrating your uncle's moderation. However, it is quite clear that your uncle's views tend to be further outside the mainstream, just not consistently in one direction.

The lesson is this: Attempting to describe Americans' general political views across multiple issues can yield misleading pictures of where they really stand relative to their representatives. Most Americans are simply not ideologically consistent enough that ideological labels such as "conservative," "liberal," or "moderate" accurately describe them.[3]

So, how common are the "crazy uncles" and how common are the real moderates in the public? In this survey, I sought to measure support for extreme policies, like establishing a maximum income or banning the sale of birth control pills. I presented Americans with questions on a dozen different issues. Each question had seven possible responses—a couple of extreme response options on either side (let's call these

---

[3]Andrew Gelman, "Political Values and Scientific Attitudes," *The Monkey Cage*, December 2, 2013. http://www.washingtonpost.com/blogs/monkey-cage/wp/2013/12/02/political-values-and-scientific-attitudes/.

points −3, −2, 2, and 3), options representing the parties' general positions (at −1 and 1), and a moderate option (at 0). I also sent this survey to a sample of state legislators.

How often do members of the public support more extreme policies than legislators?

The most common way of looking at the data is presented in Figure 15.[4] Here, I averaged each person's responses across multiple issues to generate a summary of each person's overall views (or "ideology") and then calculated how extreme their views appeared overall. For example, your uncle would score as a 3 on the gay rights question and a −3 on the health-care question, meaning he would average out to a 0, or "moderate on average." The congressperson who scores at the Republican position of 1 on both issues appears more conservative—and more extreme—with an average position of 1. Looking at the data this way, the figure suggests that the public is much more moderate than legislators, as political scientists increasingly report.

But what if we do not treat Americans as ideologues and instead look at their views on each issue, one by one?

---

[4] Joseph Bafumi and Michael C. Herron, "Leapfrog Representation and Extremism: A Study of American Voters and Their Members in Congress," *American Political Science Review* 104, 3 (2010): 519–42; Walter J. Stone and Elizabeth N. Simas, "Candidate Valence and Ideological Positions in U.S. House Elections," *American Journal of Political Science* 54, 2 (2010): 371–88; Joshua D. Clinton, "Representation in Congress: Constituents and Roll Calls in the 106th," *The Journal of Politics* 68, 2 (2006): 397–409; Boris Shor and Jon C. Rogowski, "Congressional Voting by Spatial Reasoning, 2000-2010," *Washington University St. Louis*, May 2012. http://www.pages.wustl.edu/files/pages/imce/rogowski/spatial_voting_2012.pdf.

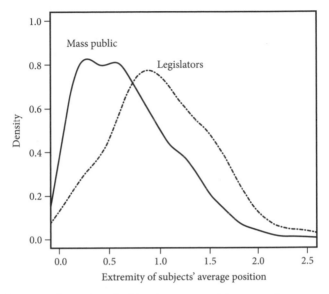

Figure 15 Extremity of subjects' average position across issues.

To calculate Figure 16, I considered how far from the middle each respondent's views typically were on each issue. For example, if your uncle answered a 3 and a −3, he would be on average 3 away from the middle. However, when his congressperson answers at 1 on both, it identifies his responses as "on average 1 away from the middle," now correctly capturing the fact that his positions tend to be more moderate than your uncle's, even though he is more ideologically consistent. When we compute extremity this way, the new conventional wisdom is upended: The

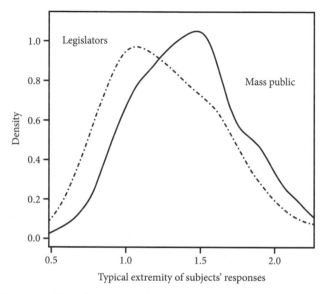

Figure 16 Typical extremity of subjects' responses.

public appears likelier to support extreme policies than legislators.

Indeed, although each of the parties is out of step with public sentiment on some issues, neither consistently out-flanks the public. For example, about 40 percent of Americans seem to have more liberal positions on tax policies than most Democratic elected officials, while much of the public would also prefer more conservative policies on immigration and abortion than most Republican elected officials would endorse.

There is a similar inversion of conventional wisdom when it comes to the attitudes of the most politically engaged Americans, who are often blamed for pulling politics to the extremes. When I examine whether more engaged individuals are more likely to support extreme policies on any given issue, they actually appear slightly *less* likely to do so. (For those interested in the details, the paper dives into these issues at greater length.)[5]

Many political observers have the sense that something has gone awry in American politics, and the metaphor of extreme elites spurning a moderate public is understandably appealing. They may be right to worry that American politicians are more partisan and less responsive than in decades past, that interest groups have succeeded in countermanding majority will in many instances, or that each of the parties is out of step on some issues. However, concerns about a wholesale "disconnect" between extreme elite positions and moderate public opinion may be overstated.

In fact, the Americans who we often call moderates may be *less* likely to adopt moderate positions on any given issue. These Americans appear more aptly described as "conflicted," agreeing with each party on some issues and *more* extreme than either party on others.

Overall labels like "moderates," "liberals," or "extremists" are often not able to describe individual Americans' opinions at all—and, when we do analyze public opinion

---

[5]David E. Broockman, "Approaches to Studying Representation," *University of California, Berkley*, September 22, 2014. http://www.ocf.berkeley.edu/~broockma/broockman_approaches_to_studying_representation.pdf.

in ideological terms like these, we are likely to be led astray. As the relationship between mass opinion and politicians' actions differs a great deal by issue, better understanding about what may ail American politics may require attending to the unique politics each issue presents.[6]

Discussion questions

- What does it mean to say someone is "ideologically consistent"?
- Why does the author believe that averaging issue positions creates a misleading measure?
- Why does it matter if the public is more or less extreme than elected officials?

Further reading

Broockman, David E. (2014), "Approaches to Studying Representation," University of California, Berkeley. http://www.ocf.berkeley.edu/~broockma/broockman_approaches_to_studying_representation.pdf

[6]Jeffrey R. Lax and Justin H. Phillips, "The Democratic Deficit in the States," *American Journal of Political Science* 65, 1 (2012): 148–66.

8

Party polarization is making us more prejudiced

Lilliana Mason

In media coverage of politics, most partisan conflicts tend to be described as a fight about something substantive. The October 2013 government shutdown was about Obamacare. The 2010 election was about government spending, perhaps. But even salient partisan battles are not entirely about specific policy questions. Party polarization is also a social process, where partisans are driven by a growing team spirit that is disconnected from policy considerations.

In Chapter 4, Thomas Carsey and Geoffrey Layman discussed the power of our partisan identities to drive our policy attitudes. But as some of my recent research has found, our political identities can do a lot more than simply affecting our political beliefs.[1]

[1]Lilliana Mason (2015), "'I Disrespectfully Agree': The Differential Effects of Partisan Sorting on Social and Issue Polarization." *American Journal of Political Science*, 59, 1 (2015): 128–45.

I examined ANES data and found that partisan and ideological identities (and particularly the alignment between the two) are capable of powerfully driving what I call social polarization.[2] This type of polarization is made up of three major effects, each of which occurs independently of our policy beliefs. No matter what we believe about policy, we are growing prejudiced against our opponents, more activist, and more emotionally volatile.

First, as our partisan and ideological identities grow stronger and more aligned (see Chapter 6), we become more prejudiced against our partisan opponents. These effects have already been observed by social psychologists for many other kinds of identities. When we have strong and overlapping identities, we are biased against people who are not in our groups. We stereotype them, we dislike them, and we evaluate them unfairly.[3] The stronger our identities, the stronger our response to intergroup rivalry.[4] But I find that these processes operate for partisan identities as well.

---

[2]"American National Election Studies," *American National Election Studies*, accessed September 23, 2014. http://www.electionstudies.org/.

[3]Shanto Iyengar, Gaurav Sood, and Yphtach Lelkes, "Affect, Not Ideology: A Social Identity Perspective on Polarization," *Public Opinion Quarterly* 76, 3 (2012): 405–31; Elmar Schlueter, Peter Schmidt, and Ulrich Wagner, "Disentangling the Causal Relations of Perceived Group Threat and Outgroup Derogation: Cross-national Evidence from German and Russian Panel Surveys," *European Sociological Review* 24, 5 (2008): 567–81; Muzafer Sherif, O. J. Harvey, B. Jack White, William R. Hood, and Carolyn W. Sherif, *The Robbers Cave Experiment: Intergroup Conflict and Cooperation* (Norman: The University of Oklahoma, 1961).

[4]Leonie Huddy, "From Social to Political Identity: A Critical Examination of Social Identity Theory," *Political Psychology* 22, 1 (2001): 127–56.

Second, I find that strong and aligned political identities compel people into political activism, including attending political rallies, influencing other people's votes, volunteering or donating to parties or candidates, and wearing a candidate's button or sticker. Again, this effect is independent of people's actual policy positions. We are getting involved in politics mostly because we want our team to win, and only slightly to get the policy outcomes we like. Here as well, this result has been found by social psychologists studying other identities. For example, one study by Marga DeWeerd and Bert Klandermans found that when farmers felt strongly connected to their farmer identity they were more likely to participate in a political protest.[5] The farmers who did not think of themselves as farmers had just as much to gain from protesting. But they did not have a strong identity to push them along.

Third, people with strong and overlapping political identities are much more likely to be angry at the opposing party's presidential candidate during every presidential election. Even when strongly partisan and ideologically sorted people do not care much about political issues, they are still a very angry group of people.

All three of these results come directly out of our psychological attachments to our social groups. In short, what others have shown for other social groups holds for partisan groups as well.

---

[5]Marga De Weerd and Bert Klandermans, "Group Identification and Political Protest: Farmers' Protest in the Netherlands," *European Journal of Social Psychology* 29, 8 (1999): 1073–95.

Research in social psychology has found that when one of our social groups (say, Republicans) is in conflict with another group (Democrats), that group identity becomes more central to our idea of who we are. The more intense the competition between the parties, the more we respond to politics as members of partisan teams, not as citizens (see Chapter 11).

A threat to our group's status also causes us to think, feel, and act defensively. We are hard-wired to feel like losers if our group loses, and to feel like winners if our group wins.[6] We are also hard-wired to avoid feeling like losers if at all possible. When the prestige of one of our groups is under threat (something which happens constantly in partisan politics), we—often unconsciously—lash out at our opponents. This is social polarization. We are a nation of partisans who are prejudiced against each other, active just for the sake of winning, and increasingly angry. We might believe that we are responding to specific policy disputes, but to a very real extent we are also being driven by an automatic, basic need to defend our social group.

To make things worse, when one social identity is aligned with another (i.e. Democrat and liberal), those identities grow stronger still. People with highly aligned identities have proved to be more intolerant, biased, and angry than those with cross-cutting identities, such as being a conservative and

[6]Henri Tajfel, and John Turner (1979), "An Integrative Theory of Group Conflict," In *The Social Psychology of Intergroup Relations* (William G. Austin and Stephen Worchel, eds.), Monterey, CA: Brooks/Cole, pp. 33–47.

a Democrat.[7] Unfortunately, in recent decades we have seen what political scientists call partisan sorting (see Chapter 6). Democrats have grown more liberal and Republicans have grown more conservative. The parties have also moved further apart on race and religion (see Chapter 12). In other words, America has gone from being a nation of cross-cutting political identities to a nation of highly aligned political identities. This further reinforces social polarization. Just by moving a few potent social identities into line behind our parties, we have made the competition between the parties more fierce, as partisans have more identities to defend in every political contest. Cue even more prejudice, activism, and anger.

Finally, my research has shown that political identities drive social polarization faster than they polarize our policy opinions. This leaves us with a nation of partisans who are acting like they disagree much more than they really do. And they are doing it with all the rationality, reserve, and emotional composure of a rabid sports fan at a championship game. It does not matter whether we agree or disagree, and it does not really matter what the substance of the dispute is. We just want our side to win.[8]

The more sorted and powerful our political identities become, the less capable we are of treating our political

[7] Marilynn B. Brewer, "Social Identity Complexity," *Personality and Social Psychology Review* 6, 2 (2002): 88–106.
[8] Henri Tajfel, M. G. Billig, R. P. Bundy, and Claude Flament, "Social Categorization and Intergroup Behaviour," *European Journal of Social Psychology* 1, 2 (1971): 149–78.

opponents with fairness and equanimity. Team victory eventually trumps the policy outcomes at the heart of governing. This means that no matter what the political debate of the day is officially about, it is rooted in the partisan bias, eager action, and exaggerated anger that come directly out of our political identities.

Discussion questions

- What does the author mean by "social polarization" and how is this different from how other authors have used "polarization"?

- According to the author, why is winning and losing important in political attitudes?

Further reading

Mason, Lilliana (2015), "'I Disrespectfully Agree': The Differential Effects of Partisan Sorting on Social and Issue Polarization." *American Journal of Political Science,* 59, 1 (2015): 128–45.

9

Politics stops at the water's edge? Not recently

Robert J. Lieber

Does polarization in domestic politics affect foreign policy as well? There is a long-standing belief that it should not. A classic statement of that view can be found in the widely cited words of a leading Republican senator in the early days of the Cold War. Speaking in 1947, Michigan Senator Arthur Vandenberg, the influential chairman of the Foreign Relations Committee, provided key support to Democratic president Harry S. Truman and admonished his colleagues that "we must stop partisan politics at the water's edge." And in practice, when it comes to military intervention, both the urgency of events and rally-round-the-flag effects are often conducive to wider support within Congress and among the general public. Thus Gallup has found that in 10 conflicts over the past 2 decades, initial public approval averaged 68 percent.[1]

[1]Andrew Dugan, "U.S. Support for Action in Syria is Low vs. Past Conflicts," Gallup, September 6, 2013.

But, with the passage of time, and especially if results fall short of initial expectations, party differences over foreign policy tend to widen, both because of disagreements over the issues at stake and as a result of elite leadership.[2] As evidence of this, those who identify as Democrats are much more inclined to support the foreign policies of a Democratic president, and Republicans are likely to take cues from a Republican occupying the White House. In today's polarized climate, politics can be delayed at the water's edge, but it certainly does not stop for long.

Iraq provides a dramatic case in point. At first the intervention received broad support. On October 10–11, 2002, the House and the Senate passed resolutions authorizing President George W. Bush to use armed force in Iraq. The measure received overwhelming Republican Party support, although a majority of Senate Democrats also voted in favor (29-21), with most presidential aspirants (Sens. Hillary Rodham Clinton, Joseph R. Biden Jr., and John F. Kerry) voting yes. There was stronger Democratic opposition in the House, but nearly 40 percent of House Democrats did support the resolution. Public opinion was favorable as well. Less than a month before the outbreak of war, a Gallup poll found 59 percent of the public supporting military action, and shortly after the start of the conflict on March 20, 2003,

[2]Adam J. Berinsky, *In Time of War: Understanding American Public Opinion from World War II to Iraq* (Chicago: The University of Chicago Press Books, 2009).

a Pew poll found 72 percent of the public describing the use of force as the right decision.[3]

With time, rising casualties, no clear end in sight, and sharply polarized views of President George W. Bush, opinion about the Iraq war shifted, becoming less favorable and increasingly polarized. The extent of partisan differences was stunningly apparent in a *New York Times*-CBS poll of delegates to the 2008 Democratic and Republican national conventions. On the question of whether the United States "did the right thing in taking military action against Iraq," 80 percent of Republican delegates and 70 percent of Republican voters agreed. In stark contrast, only 14 percent of Democratic voters responded positively and just 2 percent of Democratic delegates did.[4]

These figures document not only wide public disagreement, but an even more stunning gap among political elites. Moreover, the near-complete absence of support for the Iraq war among Democratic delegates suggests the demise of the moderate to conservative current within the Democratic Party as exemplified by the political marginalization and retirement of former senator Joseph I. Lieberman (I-Conn.). Whether the result of beliefs, war weariness, or partisan sorting, these figures suggest that in foreign policy at least, political

[3]Pew Research Center, "Public Attitudes toward the War in Iraq: 2003-2008," http://www.pewresearch.org/2008/03/19/public-attitudes-toward-the-war-in-iraq-20032008/.
[4]See: http://www.nytimes.com/imagepages/2008/09/01/us/politics/20080901_POLL_GRAPHIC.html.

polarization may be reasonably symmetric. That stands in contrast to the recent APSA report's conclusion that—in the words of Nolan McCarty—"despite the widespread belief that both parties have moved to the extremes, the movement of the Republican Party to the right accounts for most of the divergence between the two parties" (see Chapter 1).

Since the withdrawal of American troops in 2011, Iraq has been in the headlines far less frequently. Syria is, however, and in the fall of 2013, partisan differences became evident over the possible US use of force there. This time, party positions on intervention were reversed, although the differences have been less dramatic than over Iraq. In a Gallup poll taken on September 3–4, 2013, at a time when President Obama appeared to be proposing action, Republicans opposed a military strike (31 percent in favor, 58 percent against).[5] Their responses were close to those of the public as a whole (36 percent in favor, 51 percent against), while Democrats remained divided (45 percent vs. 43 percent). On the whole, these results reflect a reaction to 12 years of military involvement in the region as well as the consequences and costs, human and material, of those commitments. At the same time, the differences between Democrats and Republicans are influenced by the fact that Obama rather than George W. Bush occupies the White House.

Over the decades, support for foreign military intervention has tended to be cyclical. Public support often declines after wars, as it did following World War I, World War II,

---

[5]Dugan, "U.S. Support for Action in Syria is Low vs. Past Conflicts," 2013.

Korea, and Vietnam, and as now appears to be the case in regard to Afghanistan, Iraq, and Libya. Indeed, Afghanistan is considered the most unpopular of all recent American conflicts. A late December CNN/Opinion Research poll found public support for that war having dropped to 17 percent, a figure lower even than for Iraq and Vietnam at their most unpopular moments.[6]

Nonetheless, and as in the past, foreign policy elites do remain more supportive of the United States continuing to play an active role in world affairs than does the public at large. A major opinion study by the Pew Research Center for the People and the Press in collaboration with the Council on Foreign Relations (CFR) found 51 percent of the public taking the view that the United States does too much in helping solve world problems, while just 17 percent saw involvement as too little. By contrast, CFR respondents (a group encompassing foreign policy experts and practitioners) gave virtually opposite answers, with 21 percent saying too much and 41 percent too little.[7] Eventually, as the memory of recent conflicts recedes, and with new threats and challenges, public opinion will evolve yet again. At the same time, partisan loyalties and presidential politics will continue to manifest themselves. In short, politics does not stop at the water's edge.

[6] Aaron Blake, "Afghanistan War more Unpopular than Vietnam," Washington Post, December 30, 2013.
[7] Pew Research Center, "Public Sees U.S. Power Declining as Support for Global Engagement Slips," December 3, 2013.

Discussion question

- What does it mean to say that "politics stops at the water's edge," and why does this saying no longer necessarily hold in American politics?

Further reading

Berinsky, Adam J. (2009), *In Time of War: Understanding American Public Opinion from World War II to Iraq*. Chicago: The University of Chicago Press Books.

Why are we polarized?

10

The two key factors behind our polarized politics

Jeff Stonecash

The political parties in Congress are deeply polarized[1] as are also voters.[2] Evaluation of presidential job performance is increasingly driven by party identification.[3] The percentage of voters choosing to identify with a party is increasing, and those who identify with a party are consistently voting for the candidates of their party. What is driving this division and how did we arrive at this situation? While some commentators single out gerrymandering, Tea Party "birthers," and machinations by figures like the Koch brothers, these explanations miss the point. The sources of polarization are substantive, long-developing, and unlikely to disappear soon.

---

[1]Nolan McCarty, Keith T. Poole, and Howard Rosenthal, *Polarized America: The Dances of Ideology and Unequal Riches* (Cambridge: The MIT Press, 2008).
[2]Alan I. Abramowitz, *The Polarized Public: Why American Government Is so Dysfunctional* (Upper Saddle River: Pearson, 2012).
[3]Gary C. Jacobson, *Divider, A, Not a Uniter* (Upper Saddle River: Pearson, 2010).

Two factors have produced our polarized politics. First, changing social conditions and government actions have combined to prompt fundamental disagreements about what and how much government should do. Second, a long-term realignment brought this debate into sharp focus. In short, today's polarization is the product of today's issues and yesterday's political realignment.

The paramount debate in American politics is how much government should help individuals and who will pay for this. This debate has grown in intensity alongside several trends. Ideas changed about how much individuals can be held responsible for their situation. More studies concluded that many people are overwhelmed by circumstances they cannot control. Inequality has steadily increased.[4] Social programs have become increasingly costly. More of the tax burden has shifted to the affluent.

The reactions of liberals and conservatives to these developments have been vastly different and those divergent reactions are driving the debate. Liberals have become steadily more supportive of programs to help people. They support expansion of an array of social programs that provide benefits—disability benefits, Medicaid and Obamacare, grants to attend college—and higher taxes on the most affluent. Their presumption is that people have needs, opportunity has been unfairly distributed, and government is the vehicle to respond.

[4]Chad Stone, "Exploring Income Inequality, Part 1: Overview," *Center on Budget and Policy Priorities*, November 28, 2011. http://www.offthechartsblog. org/exploring-income-inequality-part-1-overview/.

Conservatives have reacted by gradually becoming more adamant that government is doing too much. They still see individualism as central to how America should operate. They argue that a concern for expanding opportunity has morphed into untouchable entitlements.[5] They see the emergence of welfare and other social programs as destructive of what made America successful.[6] Their central concern is that government is coming to support too many people, creating dependency rather than hard-working individuals.[7] In this view, the reason many people are failing is because they are losing the inclination to adopt the behaviors that help people achieve.[8]

Furthermore, these programs are increasingly paid for by those who achieve. The percentage of federal income tax revenues from the top 10 percent has steadily increased, creating a more progressive income tax system.[9] They also argue that when the distribution of the benefits of social programs is included, the overall impact of the tax system is now significantly redistributive. The position of stopping tax increases has become entrenched, and no

[5]Stone, "Exploring Income Inequality, Part 1: Overview," 2011.

[6]Charles Murray, *Losing Ground: American Social Policy, 1950-1980, 10th Anniversary Edition* (New York: Basic Books, 1994).

[7]"Special Topic—A Nation of Takers," *American Enterprise Institute*, accessed September 23, 2014. http://www.aei.org/topic/nation-of-takers.

[8]Charles Murray, *Coming Apart: The State of White America, 1960-2010* (New York: Crown Forum, 2013).

[9]Scott A. Hodge, "Putting a Face on America's Tax Returns: A Chart Book," *Tax Foundation,* October 21, 2013. http://www.taxfoundation.org/slideshow/putting-face-americas-tax-returns.

Republican in Congress has voted for a tax increase since 1993.[10]

The result is a fundamental difference between liberals and conservatives regarding how much government should help people.[11] It is the basis for an increase in ideological conflict and creates intense battles over the legitimacy and funding of social programs.[12] The battle has involved changes in welfare programs, limits on the ability to declare personal bankruptcy, tax cuts, and Obamacare. It is not a debate that is likely to go away because none of the precipitating conditions are likely to change in the near future.

Washington is different from 30, 40, and 50 years ago because the substance of the debate and the social and policy conditions are different. Government does more. Tax burdens are distributed differently. There are those who suggest that policy differences are largely the same and the only difference over time is that voters have sorted themselves out more between the two parties.[13] To make that argument is to dismiss the policy developments of the last 50 years and to

[10]Binyamin Appelbaum, "How Party of Budget Restraint Shifted to 'No New Taxes,' Ever," *The New York Times*, December 22, 2012. http://www.nytimes.com/2012/12/23/us/politics/how-party-of-budget-restraint-shifted-to-no-new-taxes-ever.html?_r=2&.

[11]Morgan Marietta, *A Citizen's Guide to American Ideology: Conservatism and Liberalism in Contemporary Politics* (London: Routledge, 2012).

[12]Abramowitz, *The Polarized Public*, 2012; Thomas Byrne Edsall, *The Age of Austerity: How Scarcity Will Remake American Politics* (New York: Anchor, 2012).

[13]Fiorina et al., *Culture War? The Myth of a Polarized America*, 2010; Matthew Levendusky, *The Partisan Sort: How Liberals Became Democrats and Conservatives Became Republicans* (Chicago: University of Chicago Press, 2009).

assume the context of the 1950s and 1960s still prevails. The debate is more intense because the stakes have changed.

How did we get here? As recently as the late 1990s, a central theme was that elections were candidate-centered, and few would have expected the level of party discipline in Congress that we see now.[14] In reality, the separation of congressional results from presidential results was temporary.[15] A long-term realignment was occurring.[16]

Beginning in the 1960s, Republicans began to pursue a more conservative electoral base, particularly in the South. Democrats, based for a century in the South, pursued a more liberal base, which was primarily in the North and in urban areas. Presidential results changed faster than congressional results, creating the appearance of candidate-centered elections for Congress.[17] Eventually the South veered toward the Republicans and the Northeast toward the Democrats.[18] This long-term realignment produced the pattern shown in Figure 17. It displays the correlation

[14]Martin P. Wattenberg, *The Rise of Candidate-Centered Politics: Presidential Elections of 1980s* (Cambridge: Harvard University Press, 1992).

[15]Jeffrey M. Stonecash, *Reassessing the Incumbency Effect* (Cambridge: Cambridge University Press, 2008).

[16]David Karol, *Party Position Change in American Politics: Coalition Management* (Cambridge: Cambridge University Press, 2009).

[17]Jeffrey M. Stonecash, *Party Pursuits and the Presidential-House Election Connection, 1900-2008* (Cambridge: Cambridge University Press, 2013).

[18]Byron E. Shafer and Richard Johnston, *The End of Southern Exceptional: Class, Race, and Partisan Change in the Postwar South* (Cambridge: Harvard University Press, 2009); Howard L. Reiter and Jeffrey M. Stonecash, *Counter Realignment: Political Change in the Northeastern United States* (Cambridge: Cambridge University Press, 2011).

between presidential and House results and the presence of split outcomes from 1900–2012. Beginning in the 1970s, the correlation between presidential and House voting increased sharply, and the number of districts who split their vote for president and House declined. By 2012, only 7 percent of districts had split outcomes.

For a long time, Republican House candidates in particular could not capitalize on presidential results in districts. As late as 1990 Republicans won only 51 percent of the House districts George H. W. Bush won in 1988. In 1994 the party made major gains and in 1996 it won 89 percent of the seats won by its presidential candidate. In 2012 Republicans won 96 percent of these seats. After decades when many Republican House members had to worry that their electoral base was not sympathetic to conservative positions, they now can count on a base that is truly supportive.

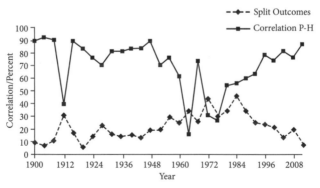

Figure 17 Correlation of Republican Presidential-House Election Results and Percent Split Outcomes, 1900–2012.

Polarization thus derives from the combination of a growing debate about the role of government and a realignment that has brought Republicans a more secure base. Each party may have a few extremists, but in large part they are representing their constituents. The current polarization is not because Republicans have gone off the deep end, but because of fundamental policy disagreements, prompted by the central questions facing American society.[19]

So long as those issues remain unresolved, the polarization that they foster is likely to be with us as well.

Discussion question

- There have always been ideological differences over the size of government. What does the author say is new in this debate that is driving polarization?

Further reading

Reiter, Howard L. and Jeffrey M. Stonecash (2011), *Counter Realignment: Political Change in the Northeastern United States*. Cambridge: Cambridge University Press.

---

[19]Thomas E. Mann and Norman J. Ornstein, *It's Even Worse Than it Looks: How the American Constitutional System Collided with the New Politics of Extremism* (New York: Basic Books, 2013).

11

American politics is more competitive than ever, and that is making partisanship worse

Frances E. Lee

The closeness of today's party competition is decidedly not normal in American politics. In fact, the last three decades have seen the longest period of near parity in party competition for control of national institutions since the Civil War.

Figure 18 illustrates this reality. It displays a simple index of two-party competition at the national level for every Congress between 1861 and the present. The measure is just the average of the Democratic Party's share of the two-party presidential vote, House seats, and Senate seats. I then display the index's divergence from a 50–50 balance for each decade. The closer the bar to zero, the more competitive the decade. Democratic-leaning eras are shown in gray, Republican-leaning eras in black. Dotted bars indicate evenly matched competition.

As is evident from this measure, the period since 1980 stands out as the longest sustained period of competitive balance between the parties since the Civil War. Our politics is distinctive for its narrow and switching national majorities.

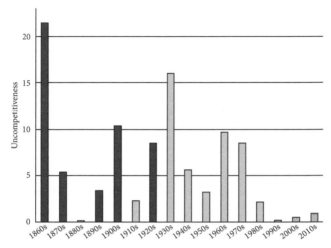

Figure 18 Index of two-party competition, 1861–2013. Zero means evenly balanced competition. Distance from 0 means a tilt toward one party, with Republican eras in black, Democratic eras in gray. The dotted gray indicates a difference of <1.

Nearly every recent election has held out the possibility of a shift in party control of one institution or another. Looking back, the period most similar to the present was the Gilded Age (1876–96), another era of close and alternating party majorities, as well as of ferocious party conflict.

Competition fuels party conflict by raising the political stakes of every policy dispute. When control of national institutions hangs in the balance, no party wants to grant political legitimacy to its opposition by voting for the measures it champions. After all, how can a party wage an effective campaign after supporting or collaborating with its opposition on public policy? Instead, parties in a competitive environment will want to amplify the differences voters perceive between themselves and their opposition. They will continually strive to give voters an answer to the key question: "Why should you support us instead of them?" Even when the parties do not disagree in substantive terms, they still have political motivations to actively seek and find reasons to oppose one another. In an environment as closely competitive as the present, even small political advantages can be decisive in winning or losing institutional majorities.

During the long years of Democratic dominance following the New Deal, politics was less contentious in part because the national political stakes were so much lower. Democrats did not perceive themselves in danger of losing their outsized majorities. The "permanent minority" Republicans did not see a path to majority status. In such an environment, members of the minority party were more willing to bargain over legislative initiatives in which they would vote "yea" in exchange for substantive policy concessions, because such support did not grant political legitimacy to an opposition that they hoped to vanquish at the next election. Meanwhile, members of the majority party were more willing to fight about public policies internally among themselves, rather than attempting to close ranks against an opponent that had little perceived chance of winning power.

Competition for power, not only ideological polarization, contributes to our confrontational contemporary politics.[1]

---

[1] Lee, *Beyond Ideology*, 2009.

As Sarah Binder and I emphasize in our contribution to the recent APSA Report on Negotiating Agreement in Politics, today's political context disincentivizes successful bipartisan negotiation.[2] The permanent campaign and politicians' continual eye on the next election pervasively discourage efforts to work across party lines.

In short, the difficulties of the present moment stem from politicians' quest for partisan advantage in an extraordinarily competitive context, as well as from their opposing political ideologies.

Discussion question

- If one party gained a dominant majority in Congress and party competition for control of national institutions declined, do you think that would decrease polarization? Why or why not?

Further reading

Binder, Sarah A. and Frances E. Lee (2013), "Making Deals in Congress," in Jane Mansbridge and Cathie Jo Martin (eds), *APSA Task Force on Negotiating Agreement in Politics*. Washington, DC: American Political Science Association, pp. 54–72. Chapter 3.

---

[2]"Task Force on Negotiating Agreement in Politics," *American Political Science Association*, accessed September 24, 2014. http://www.apsanet.org/content_88045.cfm.

12

How race and religion have polarized American voters

Alan I. Abramowitz

The rise of polarized politics in Washington is a direct result of profound changes that have taken place in American society and culture over several decades. These changes include a dramatic increase in racial and ethnic diversity and a deepening divide over religion and moral values. As a result of these societal and cultural shifts, the electoral coalitions supporting the two major parties have become increasingly distinctive. Democratic and Republican voters today are far more divided by race, religious beliefs, ideological orientations, and policy preferences than in the past.

Contrary to the views of those who see polarization as almost entirely an elite phenomenon, the deep divide between the parties in Washington and in many state capitals is largely due to the fact that Democratic and Republican elected officials represent electoral coalitions that differ sharply in their social characteristics and political orientations. The roots of polarization are in our changing society—and above all the growing racial and ethnic diversity of the American population.

Due to large-scale immigration from Latin America and Asia and higher fertility rates among nonwhites, the racial and ethnic makeup of the American population has undergone a major transformation since the 1960s. Nonwhites comprise a growing share of the overall population and of eligible voters. This demographic shift has had very different effects on the two major parties, however.

The impact of growing racial and ethnic diversity on the American electorate and on the composition of the Democratic and Republican electoral coalitions is readily evident in Figure 19. Not only has the nonwhite share of

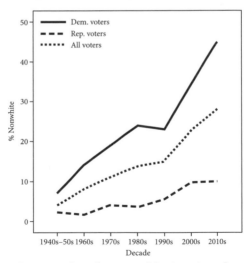

Figure 19 Growing ethnic diversity of the American electorate.

voters in presidential elections quintupled since the 1950s—and more than doubled since the 1990s—but the racial divide between the Democratic and Republican electoral coalitions has widened dramatically.

Before the 1965 Voting Rights Act resulted in the rapid enfranchisement of African-American voters in the southern states, both parties' electoral coalitions were overwhelmingly white. Today, the Republican electoral coalition remains overwhelmingly white. Nonwhites made up only 10 percent of Romney voters according to the 2012 national exit poll. But the nonwhite share of Democratic voters has increased fairly steadily since the 1960s and that trend has accelerated since 1992. Nonwhites comprised 45 percent of all Obama voters in 2012, and a majority of Obama voters under age 40.

The political significance of increasing racial diversity reflects the reality that, despite much progress in race relations over the past half-century, American society remains deeply divided along racial lines. In many ways, the United States is still a segregated and unequal society. African-Americans and Latinos continue to experience significantly worse health outcomes, poorer educational and job opportunities, inferior housing, higher unemployment, and lower incomes than white Americans. They are also much more likely to encounter hostility and prejudice in their interactions with public and private bureaucracies.[1] These differences in life experiences and opportunities are reflected in sharply

[1] Eduardo Bonilla-Silva, *Racism without Racists: Color-Blind Racism and the Persistence of Racial Inequality in America* (Lanham: Rowman & Littlefield Publishers, 2009).

differing views on issues such as taxation, spending on social services and the proper role of government—as well as major differences in party identification and voting behavior.[2]

The growing dependence of Democratic candidates and officeholders on nonwhite voters, along with a Republican strategy of appealing to white voters unhappy with the Democratic Party's racial and economic liberalism, has contributed to an ideological and regional realignment within the white electorate. Conservative whites in the South and elsewhere have moved increasingly into the Republican camp, while moderate-to-liberal whites in the Northeast, Midwest, and Pacific states have moved increasingly into the Democratic camp.

There is every reason to expect these trends will continue. Census data indicate that the nonwhite share of newly eligible voters will continue to grow for many years. Yet despite the threat that this trend poses to the future viability of the Republican Party in national elections, the influence of the ultra-conservative, anti-immigration Tea Party movement makes it unlikely that the GOP will be able to successfully appeal to this growing nonwhite electorate. As a result, the racial divide between the parties' electoral coalitions is likely to increase over the next several election cycles.

Race has certainly not been the only factor behind rising partisan polarization. Another crucial component of the

[2]Donald R. Kinder and Allison Dale-Riddle, *The End of Race? Obama, 2008, and Racial Politics in America* (New Haven: Yale University Press, 2012); Michael Tesler and David O. Sears, *Obama's Race: The 2008 Election and the Dream of a Post-Racial America* (Chicago: University of Chicago Press, 2010).

ideological realignment of the past thirty years has been a growing religious divide between the parties. This is not the traditional divide between Protestants and Catholics that dominated American politics in much of the country during the first half of the twentieth century. Instead, it is a divide between the religiously observant and nonobservant.

In addition to appealing to white voters unhappy with the racial liberalism of the Democratic Party, Republican leaders starting with Ronald Reagan sought to appeal to evangelicals and other religious conservatives within the white electorate who were unhappy about the Supreme Court's *Roe v. Wade* decision legalizing abortion and other perceived threats to traditional values. The result may not have been a "culture war," but it certainly was a widening partisan divide between religious and nonreligious white voters, as Figure 20 shows.

The movement of religiously observant white voters into the Republican camp accelerated after the GOP made circumventing *Roe v. Wade* a key plank of its national party platform in 1980. And the partisan divide between observant and nonobservant white voters continued to widen in the 1990s and 2000s as gay rights and same-sex marriage became salient issues.

By 2012, 69 percent of white voters who reported attending religious services at least once per week identified with the Republican Party compared with only 41 percent of white voters who reported rarely or never attending religious services—the largest divide ever recorded. Some 75 percent of religiously observant whites voted for Mitt Romney in 2012 compared with only 46 percent of nonobservant whites.

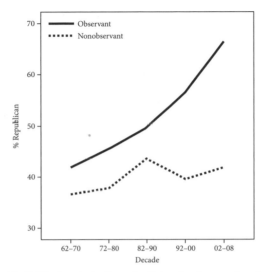

Figure 20 Political polarization of religiously observant and nonobservant people.

Much attention has been paid by political commentators to the potential impact of growing income inequality on partisan polarization. When it comes to explaining partisan polarization in the contemporary American electorate, however, income differences appear to play a much smaller role than either race or religion. According to data from the American National Election Study, the correlation between family income and party identification among all voters in 2012 was a very modest 0.13. As family income goes up, voters are a bit more likely to back the Republicans, but not strongly so. The correlation among white voters was meager and statistically insignificant 0.03.

As Figure 21 shows, at every level of family income, religiously observant whites were much more likely to vote for the Republican presidential candidate in 2012 than nonobservant whites. In fact, nonobservant, upper-income whites were much more likely to vote Democratic than religiously observant lower-income whites. Indeed, family income had no relationship at all with vote choice among religiously observant whites. A remarkable 80 percent of

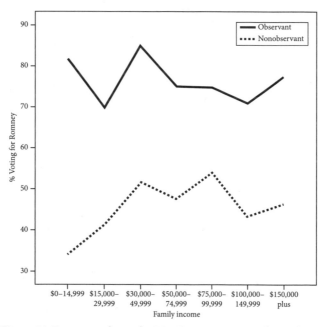

Figure 21 Income and vote for Mitt Romney among religiously observant and nonobservant people.

observant whites with family incomes below $15,000 voted for a Republican presidential candidate who famously expressed no interest in appealing to 47 percent of the electorate including, presumably, those living below the poverty line.

The 2012 election results once again revealed the existence of an electorate deeply divided by race, religion, and ideology. Those divisions are found among general election as well as primary voters. The Democratic and Republican electoral coalitions are more distinctive now in terms of social characteristics and political outlook than at any time in the past sixty years. There is no disconnect between representatives and represented—today's elite polarization is not imposed on a centrist electorate.

The deep partisan divide in Washington clearly reflects a deep partisan divide within the American electorate, and for this reason, it is unlikely to diminish any time soon.

Discussion questions

- What distinguishes the current partisan divide on religion from past divisions?
- What are some potential explanations the author might give for why there does not seem to be a partisan gap across income groups?

Further reading

Abramowitz, Alan I. (2012), *The Polarized Public: Why American Government Is so Dysfunctional*. Upper Saddle River: Pearson.

13

How ideological activists constructed our polarized parties

Hans Noel

When you think of polarization, I suspect you think that the parties have moved apart on some fixed liberal-to-conservative dimension. At best, that is a simplification. What has really happened is the party system finally catching up with the development of ideology.

That makes it look like we have *extreme* parties, but what we really have is *distinct* parties.

For one thing, the liberal-conservative conflict, in its modern form, is relatively new. A hundred years ago, party competition was intense, but it was not over the same issues. Those who were against, say, teaching evolution in schools were as often for redistributive policies as against them. Most strikingly, the progressives of the Progressive Era, who were concerned about inequality and wanted the government to intervene in the market, were generally fairly racist. Government should help out struggling white workers, progressives thought, but perhaps blacks were destined to be poor and uneducated.

This changed over the course of the first half of the twentieth century. Antiblack progressives faded, and modern liberals replaced them. They were people who were liberal on economics, liberal on race, and liberal on a lot of other things. In my new book, I look at the positions taken by political intellectuals in magazines and newspapers.[1] Among those thinkers, modern liberalism began to emerge in the early twentieth century, and modern conservatism followed in the middle of the century.

But the parties took a while to catch up to these developments in ideology. Parties are coalitions of people trying to get elected. They had built constituencies based on idiosyncratic platforms, which evolved locally in different ways. They were not ideologically distinct from one another. Northern Democrats began to represent liberal voters (and, perhaps more importantly, liberal activists). But Southern Democrats, meanwhile, had constituencies based on opposition to civil rights, but also on a commitment to the Cold War and opposition to labor unions. Southern Democrats were not just more conservative than other Democrats—they were more conservative than most Republicans.

Much has been made of the fact that many early social programs, like Medicare and Social Security, were enacted by bipartisan coalitions, while the Affordable Care Act was passed on party-line votes. This is true. But this is not because there was a great consensus on Medicare. It is

[1]Hans Noel, *Political Ideologies and Political Parties in America* (Cambridge: Cambridge University Press, 2014).

because the liberals who were for it were in both parties, and the conservatives who opposed it were also in both parties.

Ideological activists had to force the parties to change, on race, on women's rights, on defense spending, etc. And they continue to do so. Now, there are few conservative Democrats, and even fewer liberal Republicans.

Those who study voters like to call this "sorting" and that is not bad. I think polarization is a fine term, but it is polarization because the parties have aligned themselves to new poles.[2]

Discussion questions

- According to the author, what is the difference between party and ideology?
- Why do you think the author emphasizes the role of activists multiple times?

Further reading

Noel, Hans (2014), *Political Ideologies and Political Parties in America*. Cambridge: Cambridge University Press.

[2]Fiorina et al., *Culture War? The Myth of a Polarized America*, 2010.

14

How better educated whites are driving political polarization

Andrew Gelman

My area of expertise is in public opinion and voting, so I will focus on the measurement and description of polarization rather than its causes. From a public opinion perspective, one of the cleanest pieces of evidence for me is this graph of average attitudes on abortion (on a 1–4 scale, from the American National Election Study) among self-declared Democrats, Independents, and Republicans.[1]

On or about 1990, as a latter-day Virginia Woolf might say, American politics changed. I would not take the blip of the dotted line at 1990 very seriously—sampling variability and all that—but the general pattern in Figure 22 is real, and appears in all sorts of other data. In 1988 and before: zero correlations of partisanship with attitudes; since 1992, the correlations have been big and getting larger.

But, even now, we see polarization among some groups but not others. Figure 23 presents a graph made by Yair Ghitza,

[1]"American National Election Studies," *American National Election Studies*, accessed September 24, 2014. http://www.electionstudies.org/.

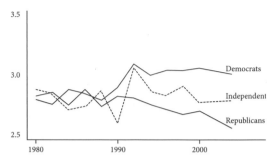

Figure 22 Development of polarization on abortion of voters by party identification. The plot displays average abortion attitudes on a 1-4 scale, with 1 representing strong opposition to abortion and 4 representing strong support of abortion rights.

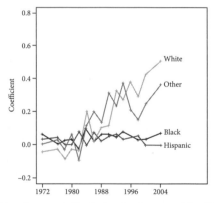

Figure 23 Development of polarization by party identification, for voters of different ethnic categories. The plot displays linear regression coefficients of abortion attitudes on party identification, with larger coefficients indicating larger differences between the parties.

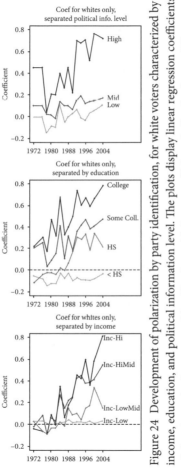

Figure 24 Development of polarization by party identification, for white voters characterized by income, education, and political information level. The plots display linear regression coefficients of abortion attitudes on party identification, with larger coefficients indicating larger differences between the parties.

showing regression coefficients predicting abortion attitudes with party identification (with coefficients smoothed via a hierarchical model). For African-Americans and Latinos, there has been a consistent near-zero correlation between partisanship and abortion attitudes. But among whites, the correlation has steadily increased since 1980.

And we can turn up the microscope even further by breaking down the whites into subgroups by income, education, or political information level (see Figure 24).

Not only is the abortion/party relationship primarily driven by whites, it is substantially stronger among white elites—that is, people with high income, education, or levels of political information.

A lot more can be said about political polarization—indeed, entire books have been written on the topic—but perhaps these graphs give a sense of the value that can be gained by making comparisons for different groups of the population, and tracing those changes over time.

Discussion questions

- What does the author mean in saying that answers become correlated with party?
- Why is that correlation important?

Further reading

Gelman, Andrew (2009), *Red State, Blue State, Rich State, Poor State: Why Americans Vote the Way they Do*. Princeton, NJ: Princeton University Press.

15

Are Fox and MSNBC polarizing America?

Matthew Levendusky

A generation ago, if ordinary Americans turned on the television at 6 p.m., they had basically one choice: to watch the evening news. They could have chosen to watch ABC, CBS, or NBC, but it would not really have mattered, because they all basically gave the same news in a similar format. Today, if they did that, they would have hundreds of options, including not just the news, but also sports, movies, re-runs, and so forth. Even within news, they have a variety of choices. Not only would they have the major network news programs, but they would have many choices on cable, most notably the partisan outlets of Fox News and MSNBC (not to mention even more choices online). This choice of explicitly partisan outlets means that individuals can choose to hear messages that reinforce their beliefs, while avoiding those from alternative points of view, which some claim leads to polarization.[1] Does this high-choice media environment, especially with its partisan outlets, polarize the public?

[1]Cass R. Sunstein, *Republic.com* (Princeton: Princeton University Press, 2001).

The evidence suggests that the media may contribute to polarization, but in a more circumscribed way than many commentators suggest. Take first the question of choice, and in particular, whether people seek out media choices that reinforce their existing beliefs. The answer is (perhaps not surprisingly) yes: Republicans are more likely to tune in to Fox News and liberals are more likely to watch MSNBC. Researchers have also found that these effects are stronger for those who are more partisan and politically involved.[2]

But there is perhaps an even more important type of selection at work. While the politically engaged can tune into Fox and MSNBC, those who dislike politics also have more options than ever for avoiding it. In lieu of the nightly news—or a televised presidential address—they can watch *Sports Center, Entertainment Tonight*, or a rerun of *The Big Bang Theory*. When confronted with a political option, they simply change the channel to something else that they find more agreeable.[3] Even the most popular cable news programs get two to three million viewers on a typical evening in a country of 300 million Americans. In earlier decades, some of those who disliked politics would have been incidentally exposed to political news and information (by, say, watching the television news at six o'clock, when there were no other options). Now that they can avoid news altogether, they know less about politics and are less likely

[2] Natalie Jomini Stroud, *Niche News: The Politics of News Choice* (Oxford: Oxford University Press, 2011).
[3] Kevin Arceneaux and Martin Johnson, *Changing Minds or Changing Channels?: Partisan News in an Age of Choice* (Chicago: University of Chicago Press, 2013).

to participate.[4] So the growth of media choice strengthens the extremes while hollowing out the center, making the electorate more divided.

But what about the effects of partisan media on those who do watch these programs? While this research tradition is still relatively young, scholars have found a number of effects: on vote choice, participation, and attitudes toward bipartisanship and compromise, among others.[5] The research looking at effects on attitudes finds that while there are effects, they are concentrated primarily among those who are already extreme.[6] This suggests that these programs contribute to polarization not by shifting the center of the ideological distribution, but rather by lengthening the tails (i.e., moving the polarized even further away from the center).

It is vital to put these effects into context. As noted above, these programs attract a small audience, but those who watch

[4]Markus Prior, *Post-Broadcast Democracy: How Media Choice Increases Inequality in Political Involvement and Polarizes Elections* (New York: Cambridge University Press, 2007).

[5]Susanna Dilliplane, "Activation, Conversion, or Reinforcement? The Impact of Partisan News Exposure on Vote Choice," *American Journal of Political Science* 58, 1 (2014): 79–94; Dan Hopkins, "How the Rise of Fox News Helped Republican Candidates," *Wonkblog*, July 7, 2013. http://www.washingtonpost.com/blogs/wonkblog/wp/2013/07/07/how-the-rise-of-fox-news-helped-republican-candidates/; Susanna Dilliplane, "All the News You Want to Hear: The Impact of Partisan News Exposure on Political Participation," *Public Opinion Quarterly* 75, 2 (2011): 287–316; Jeffrey M. Berry and Sarah Sobieraj, *The Outrage Industry: Political Opinion Media and the New Incivility* (Oxford: Oxford University Press, 2014).

[6]Matthew Levendusky, *How Partisan Media Polarize America* (Chicago: Chicago University Press, 2013).

these shows are more partisan, politically interested, and politically involved; these are the individuals who are more likely to make their voices heard in the halls of power. So to the extent that these shows matter, it is by influencing this relatively narrow audience. These programs have few direct effects on most Americans.

While scholars have learned a great deal about how media might shape polarization, there are still many questions to be answered. First, we know essentially nothing about the indirect effects of these shows: do those who watch these shows transmit some of the effects to non-watchers through discussion in social networks? Does the Rachel Maddow fan in the cubicle next to you shape your opinions by telling you what she discussed on her show last night? Second, what is the effect of these shows on the broader media agenda, and on elites? Do the frames and issues that originate on Fox or MSNBC influence the broader media agenda? If so, that is an important finding, as it shows how these networks help to shape what a wider swath of Americans see.

In general, we understand little about how news outlets influence one another, especially in a 24-hour news cycle. Some recent work suggests that these outlets (particularly Fox) have shaped the behavior of members of Congress.[7] The work discussed here has focused on the effects of cable TV news (with similar effects found previously for political talk

---

[7]Joshua Clinton and Ted Enamorado, "The National News Media's Effect on Congress: How Fox News Affected Representatives in Congress," *Journal of Politics*, 76, 4 (2014): 928–43.

radio).[8] But there is an even broader range of material on the Internet, and few works have yet explored these effects. How the Internet—and especially social media sites like Twitter and Facebook—contributes to polarization will be an important topic in the years to come.

Discussion questions

- What type of people watch cable news? Why is that important in determining its effect?
- How does the author believe that cable news might lead to polarization?

Further reading

Levendusky, Matt (2013), *How Partisan Media Polarize America*. Chicago: The University of Chicago Press.

[8]Kathleen Hall Jamieson and Joseph N. Cappella, *Echo Chamber: Rush Limbaugh and the Conservative Media Establishment* (Oxford: Oxford University Press, 2010).

16

Why you should not blame polarization on partisan news

Kevin Arceneaux

In casting about for explanations for the unprecedented level of polarization in Congress, many singled out the partisan news media. This is an understandable notion, but unlikely nonetheless. Partisan media, which reach a small slice of the electorate at any rate, emerged well after Congress began to polarize, and mainstream news media have just as much power to polarize.

The expansion of programming choices on cable television in the late 1990s made partisan news media possible. But today Americans can watch not only partisan news but hundreds of other channels, most of which are not political at all, much less partisan. As Martin Johnson and I demonstrate in our new book and discuss elsewhere, the plethora of entertainment options filters out those who are most likely to be persuaded by news shows (partisan or otherwise) and blunts the polarizing effects of partisan news on the mass public.[1]

---

[1] Arceneaux and Johnson, *Changing Minds or Changing Channels?*, 2013; Dan Kahan, "Partisan Media Are Not Destroying America," *The Cultural Cognition*

If partisan media played any role in generating polarization in Congress, it is unlikely to have done so by polarizing the mass public first. But perhaps partisan media polarize through an indirect path. Matt Levendusky makes the case that partisan news shows energize viewers, inducing them to contact members of Congress and creating the impression of a broadly polarized electorate.[2] While plausible, this scenario offers a better explanation for how partisan media may reinforce polarization rather than for how polarization came about in the first place.

For one, polarization in Congress precedes the advent of partisan media by almost two decades. Fox News appeared at the end of 1996 and was not widely available until the early 2000s. The parties in Congress began polarizing in the late 1970s. As Jonathan Ladd points out, it could just as easily be the case that a polarized Congress contributed to the demand for partisan news media.[3]

Moreover, the partisan news media were relatively one-sided until the mid-2000s, when MSNBC gravitated to the left. Fox News was the first ostensibly partisan news channel on the dial, and it reported news with a conservative slant.[4] In a working paper, Martin Johnson, Rene Lindstadt, Ryan Vander Wielen, and I use the uneven roll-out of the Fox News network to investigate its effects on congressional voting

Project, August 8, 2013. http://www.culturalcognition.net/blog/2013/8/8/partisan-media-are-not-destroying-america.html.

[2]Levendusky, *How Partisan Media Polarize America*, 2013.

[3]Jonathan M. Ladd, *Why Americans Hate the Media and How it Matters* (Princeton: Princeton University Press, 2012).

[4]Tim Groseclose and Jeffrey Milyo, "A Measure of Media Bias," *The Quarterly Journal of Economics* 120, 4 (2005): 1191–237.

behavior.[5] We find that *both* Democratic and Republican representatives located in districts that had access to Fox News were more likely to vote in line with the Republican agenda in the months just before the general election.[6] This pattern is consistent with Levendusky's argument that partisan news outlets may influence elected representatives indirectly as well as the notion that representatives themselves may treat news programming as a barometer of public opinion.

But our finding undermines the claim that partisan news media generated congressional polarization: If Fox News is pushing all members to the right, it is not polarizing them. In fact, it is entirely possible that were it not for Fox News in the 1990s, Congress would have reached today's level of polarization sooner.

Finally, many implicitly assume that partisan news is inherently more polarizing than mainstream news. The idea here is that we are what we consume. Balanced presentations of news moderate political attitudes, while partisan presentations polarize attitudes. It is an intuitive idea but not necessarily an accurate one. People are motivated to defend cherished worldviews, especially in the realm of

[5]Arceneaux, Kevin, Martin Johnson, René Lindstädt, and Ryan J. Vander Wielen. "The Influence of News Media on Political Elites: Investigating Strategic Responsiveness in Congress." American Journal of Political Science, (forthcoming).

[6]John Sides, "How Fox Made Republicans More Republican (and Democrats more Republican, Too)," *The Monkey Cage*, October 30, 2013. http://www.washingtonpost.com/blogs/monkey-cage/wp/2013/10/30/how-fox-news-made-republicans-more-republican-and-democrats-more-republican-too/.

politics.[7] Many studies illustrate that people are capable of cherry-picking the facts they wish to believe from balanced presentations.[8]

In an experiment conducted in July 2013, Martin Johnson and I compared the polarizing effects of mainstream and partisan news. We asked people about their viewing habits and political predispositions and then randomly assigned them to watch either a nonpolitical entertainment show or news story about accusations that the Obama administration meddled in IRS audits of conservative groups. Those asked to view the news story saw either one from a mainstream outlet (CBS), their side's partisan outlet (Fox for conservatives and MSNBC for liberals), or the other side's partisan outlet (Fox for liberals and MSNBC for conservatives).

After watching the program, people were asked whether the IRS audits were politically motivated or whether the IRS made an innocent mistake. The question is which program created the most polarization—that is, with conservatives taking the view that IRS audits were politically motivated and liberals taking the view that the IRS made an innocent mistake? We found that the mainstream news program was *just as polarizing* as the partisan news programs. Subjects

---

[7]Ziva Kunda, "The Case for Motivated Reasoning," *Psychological Bulletin* 108, 3 (1990): 480–98.

[8]Charles G. Lord, Lee Ross, and Mark R. Lepper, "Biased Assimilation and Attitude Polarization: The Effects of Prior Theories on Subsequently Considered Evidence," *Journal of Personality and Social Psychology* 37, 11 (1979): 2098–109; Charles S. Taber and Milton Lodge, "Motivated Skepticism in the Evaluation of Political Beliefs," *American Journal of Political Science* 50, 3 (2006): 755–69.

assigned to view the CBS story registered more polarized opinions about the IRS than those who watched the nonpolitical show.

What is more, the polarizing effects of both partisan and mainstream news shows were driven by the reactions of people who normally do not tune into news programs (unless, that is, instructed to do so by political scientists). In fact, partisan news viewers are more polarized than mainstream news viewers and entertainment program viewers to begin with. People tune into partisan news because they *are* partisans. Even without partisan news media, these individuals would likely interpret the world through a partisan lens. Those who are most likely to be polarized by exposure to news—mainstream or partisan—tend to watch something else.

The rise of partisan news media is likely a symptom, not a cause, of elite polarization. Partisan media may reinforce partisan strife, but we should look elsewhere for the ultimate cause.

Discussion questions

- Does the author agree that partisan news are significantly more polarizing than more mainstream news? Why or why not?

- The author states that Fox News may have slowed the pace of polarization. What is the basis for this assertion?

Further reading

Arceneaux, Kevin and Martin Johnson (2013), *Changing Minds or Changing Channels? Partisan News in an Age of Choice.* Chicago: The University of Chicago Press.

17

The media make us think we are more polarized than we really are

Matthew Levendusky and Neil Malhotra

Since the disputed 2000 US presidential election, there has been a surge of scholarly and popular interest in partisan political polarization. While there is a lively debate among political scientists about the extent of polarization among ordinary Americans, the mass media typically portray the country as deeply divided along partisan lines, as that makes for more exciting journalism.[1] What kinds of effects does the media's reporting of political polarization have on Americans? Are we in a self-reinforcing cycle, in which news coverage emphasizing polarization itself has a polarizing effect?

Thanks to the support of Time-sharing Experiments in the Social Sciences, we have conducted numerous surveys

---

[1]Morris P. Fiorina, Samuel J. Abrams, and Jeremy C. Pope, *Culture War? The Myth of a Polarized America* (Upper Saddle River: Pearson, 2011); Alan I. Abramowitz, *The Disappearing Center* (New Haven: Yale University Press, 2010).

of the mass public to address these questions, which are discussed in this chapter.[2] We find that the media's coverage of polarization—and the ensuing increase in perceived polarization among Americans—influences political attitudes, but in some surprising ways. Specifically, media coverage of polarization increases antipathy of the opposing party, even as it encourages moderation among those who were more moderate to begin with.

To begin, we note that there is reason to suspect that ordinary citizens think the electorate is more divided than it actually is. Work in social psychology finds that humans tend to over-estimate the distinctiveness of rival groups— men and women, blacks and whites, Israelis and Palestinians, and, in our case, Democrats and Republicans.[3] This stems from the underlying psychology of categorization: merely labeling groups makes people see them as more distinctive than they actually are. So when people think about where "Democrats" and "Republicans" stand, they will tend to place Democrats too far to the left, and Republicans too far to the right, which psychologists term "false polarization." Previous psychological studies found this

[2]Matthew S. Levendusky and Neil A. Malhotra, "The Effect of 'False' Polarization: Are Perceptions of Political Polarization Self-Fulfilling Prophecies?", Working Paper. http://www.washingtonpost.com/blogs/monkey-cage/files/2014/01/fp_writeup_oct6_for_jop.pdf.

[3]Robert J. Robinson, Dacher Keltner, Andrew Ward, and Lee Ross, "Actual Versus Assumed Differences in Construal: 'Native Realism' in Intergroup Perception and Conflict," *Journal of Personality and Social Psychology* 68, 3 (1995): 404–17; See Chapter 8.

pattern, and we find that in our data as well, as illustrated in Figure 25.[4]

The figure plots the actual distance between Republican and Democratic respondents in our surveys as measured by seven-point issue scales (the solid lines) against how our respondents perceived the divide between Republicans and Democrats (bracketed line). Across several different surveys, we find a large degree of false polarization. That is, when we ask subjects about where they think the "average Democratic

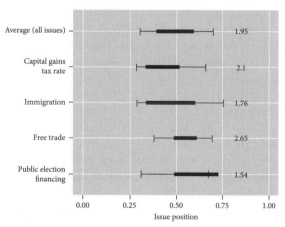

Figure 25 Comparing actual vs. perceived polarization between Democrats and Republicans.

Source: GfK/Knowledge Networks survey.

[4]Leaf Van Boven, Charles M. Judd, and David K. Sherman, "Political Polarization Projection: Social Projection of Partisan Attitude Extremity and Attitudinal Processes," *Journal of Personality and Social Psychology* 103, 1 (2012): 84–100.

voter" and "average Republican voter" stand, they think they are further apart than the average Democratic and Republican voters actually are. For example, on the issue of capital gains tax cuts, respondents think ordinary Americans are 84 percent more polarized than they actually are (see the second row of Figure 25). Because we have data from a high-quality probability sample from GfK/Knowledge Networks, these effects are not simply driven by politically motivated online survey takers, but rather reflect deeper underlying psychological tendencies.

We argue that media coverage of the electorate—which tends to emphasize polarization and discord when discussing voters (see Chapter 6)—will exacerbate false polarization. Using a population-based survey experiment, we find exactly this pattern. We randomly assigned some subjects to read media accounts of a polarized electorate and others to read accounts of a more moderate electorate. When subjects are exposed to media coverage suggesting electoral polarization and division, they perceive greater electoral polarization—as measured by where they place typical Republican and Democratic voters on issue scales (readers interested in the details of the analysis can consult our paper). This suggests that media coverage can make people think the United States is a politically polarized country even if it is not.

But what are the political implications of this false polar-ization? Counterintuitively, we find that it actually *moderates* citizens' issue positions. Most Americans support bipartisanship, compromise, and consensus, and all but the strongest partisans respond negatively to violations of these norms.[5] So when subjects read about polarized citizens who disagree with the opposition and eschew compromise and consensus, they react negatively to them. These individuals then become a sort of foil, telling subjects what *not* to believe, and as a result, subjects moderate their issue positions. Using these experimental data, we find that when subjects see polarized media coverage (relative to media coverage suggesting the electorate is more moderate), they become approximately 5 percent more moderate on traditional seven-point issue scales. False polarization is not a "self-fulfilling prophecy": the media reporting on a polarized electorate will likely not create one.

But such false polarization has a more pernicious effect as well: it increases what Shanto Iyengar and his colleagues have termed "affective polarization," or dislike for the opposing party.[6] By the same logic as above, subjects see the polarization and division depicted in the media, and they respond negatively to it, and in particular, they especially dislike members of the other party. We find, for example, that after seeing the polarized article, subjects rate the opposing party 4 degrees lower on a feeling thermometer, and they are almost 10 percent more likely to assign them the lowest rating on the feeling thermometer scale. They also report more things they dislike about the other party, and

---

[5]Amy Gutmann and Dennis Thompson, *The Spirit of Compromise: Why Governing Demands it and Campaigning Undermines it* (Princeton: Princeton University Press, 2012); Laurel Harbridge and Neil Malhotra, "Electoral Incentives and Partisan Conflict in Congress: Evidence from Survey Experiments," *American Journal of Political Science* 55, 3 (2011): 494–510.

[6]Iyengar et al., "Affect, Not Ideology," 2012, 405–31.

evaluate its members less positively on a number of different dimensions. They view their own party less favorably, too, but to a more limited extent.

We also find that there is important heterogeneity in these effects. We find that much of the attitudinal moderation occurs among those who are already moderate *ex ante*, while the affective polarization occurs among all subjects. So the end result of this process is not a nation of moderates that dislike each other, but rather, an increasingly moderate core with extreme wings, all of whom have increased antipathy for the opposition. Our findings therefore suggest that the media likely are not shrinking mass polarization, as their moderating effects are centered on those who are already middle-of-the-road. Rather, the media help to further segment and stratify the electorate into a more moderate core turned off by polarization (see Chapter 6) and a more extreme segment (see Chapter 12). Media coverage of polarization, then, has important, and nonobvious, consequences for American politics. Though it does not create a self-fulfilling prophecy, it shapes public opinion in key ways.

Discussion questions

- Why would the authors say that the false perception of polarization could be good or bad?
- The authors ask in a working paper whether a perception of polarization makes us more polarized. Why do they accept or dismiss this concern?

Further reading

Levendusky, Matthew and Neil Malhotra (2013), "The Effect of False Polarization: Are Perceptions of Political Polarization Self-Fulfilling Prophecies?" Working Paper.

Polarization abroad

18

Sure, Congress is polarized.
But other legislatures are more so

David W. Brady

While there is some disagreement in the profession of political science about how polarized the American electorate is, there is undeniably considerable polarization in the US Congress (see Chapter 1). The post-World War II period, which saw bipartisanship in foreign affairs (see Chapter 9) and domestic legislation because of the "conservative coalition" of Northern Republicans and Southern Democrats, was replaced by high levels of polarized voting beginning in the late 1970s.

How does legislative polarization as measured in the United States stack up when we look at legislative bodies in other parts of the world? Surprisingly, the answer is we are not, relatively speaking, very polarized when compared to parliamentary systems. It is thus unclear why polarization is thought to be a special problem in the United States. Moreover, polarization as measured in parliamentary systems conceals as much about disagreement as it reveals. A comparative analysis of polarization should cause us to go back to the drawing board to ask exactly why polarization is bad.

In the United Kingdom, parliament polarization scores are basically 100 percent, in that all of Labour votes against all of the Tories. In Japan, the parties of the left vote unanimously against the Liberal Democratic Party. One common measure of unified voting by parties is the Rice index of party unity, which is the absolute difference between the proportion of party members voting in favor and the proportion of members voting in opposition, multiplied by 100. In a survey of sixteen European countries plus Australia and New Zealand, which includes ninety political parties, the lowest party unity scores were 88.63 for Finland and 93.17 for New Zealand, with the average for all sixteen countries being over ninety-seven.[1] In contrast, Michael Crespin and coauthors show that over time in the US Congress, the index's high score is 66 and, even when adjusted, is in the 75 range.[2] In sum, if we compare the United States to other democracies, its polarization levels are not particularly high.

What then is there to worry about? There may be headlines in Italy and France about dysfunctional government, but they do not blame it on polarized political parties.

---

[1]Daniela Giannetti and Kenneth Benoit, *Intra-Party Politics and Coalition Government* (London: Routledge, 2009).
[2]Michael H. Crespin, David W. Rhode, and Ryan J. Vander Wielen, "Measuring Variation in Party Unity Voting: An Assessment of Agenda Effects," *Party Politics* 19, 3 (2013): 432–57.

One thing that should generate concern: do such measures of polarization tell us much about intraparty ideology or differences? The answer is that we do not know. Party unity scores, where parties of the left uniformly vote against parties of the right, could be the result of preferences or pressure. That is, the party unity scores could be the result of members agreeing with each other—having the same preferences—or the unity could be imposed by party leaders' actions such as the three-line whip in the UK House of Commons.

Research on European parties has turned to analyses of how political parties achieve unity. In a 2012 paper, Caroline Close and Lidia Lopez show that prefloor vote disagreements within the parties are a common feature of European parliamentary parties.[3] How, then, do these parties achieve such high levels of unity and party voting? It could be that they have an internal party process where, after sufficient discussion, they agree to vote for the median position, or at the other extreme it could be that the party leaders decide the policy position and enforce unified voting. We know little about this because the processes are internal to the parties—neither the process nor the enforcement mechanism is public. Contrast this to the US Congress, where all of the disputes and differences are played out in public, as in the fall 2013 case of the Tea Party and the final budget vote. In short, in the United States, we know about polarization and

---

[3]Caroline Close and Lidia Nunez Lopez, "Party Cohesion in European Legislatures: Cross-Country and Cross-Party Comparison," Working Paper. http://www.sciencespo.site.ulb.ac.be/dossiers_membres/close-caroline/fichiers/close-caroline-publication8.pdf.

internal policy differences, whereas in Europe and other democracies, we know the party's final policy position and levels of cohesion and party voting but not how the cohesion was achieved. Before we go overboard on polarization in the United States, we need a better understanding of where we stand relative to other democracies.

In addition to the difficulty of knowing how the polarized voting came about—is it from preferences, processes, or pressure?—knowing that party polarization on a left-right basis exists does not always tell you what policies will be enacted. The Bank of England, nationalized after World War II by the newly elected Labour government of Clement Atlee, was surprisingly made independent by the newly elected Blair Labour government, an act described by the May 6, 1997, "BBC On This Day" program "as the most radical shake-up in the bank's 300 year history." A left party which nationalized the bank achieved what numerous Conservative governments could not. Similarly, the recent shift by the PRI in Mexico in regard to foreign aid interests and PEMEX, the national oil company, ought to make us aware of the need to understand both policy shifts by parties and how they achieve unity in enforcing such shifts.

Discussion questions

- Is the US Congress more or less polarized than legislatures in other established democracies?
- Can polarization help us predict the kinds of policies that will be enacted by a legislature Why or why not?

Further reading

Close, Caroline and Lidia Nunez Lopez (2013), "Party Cohesion in European Legislatures: Cross-Country and Cross-Party Comparisons." Working Paper.

19

Canada is polarizing—and it is because of the parties

Richard Johnston

Over the last decade, the Canadian party system has polarized in ways that should be familiar to US observers. In this, Canada may only have joined the other Anglo-American democracies in organizing its politics around class and left-right ideology. The route by which Canada got to this point is circuitous, and it says more about the choices parties are offering voters than it does about the voters' attitudes.

Traditionally, the Canadian system was one of the *least* polarized in the world. For more than a century, it was dominated by the Liberal Party that was unabashedly centrist. The secret of Liberal success was Quebec. From the late nineteenth to the late twentieth century, that province was the pivot for government. It typically delivered almost all of its seats to the Liberals, such that Quebec alone put that party half way to a majority.

The Liberals' chief rival was a conservative party that for most of the century carried the usefully contradictory moniker of Progressive Conservative (PC). For the PCs to capture a majority, Quebec was no less critical. So although the PC candidates outside Quebec became seriously conservative in the 1970s and 1980s, strategic imperatives moderated the party's platform. Moderation of the party's position applied to the existential question of Quebec's role within Canada, but also to bread-and-butter issues, on which Quebeckers stood rather to the left of other Canadians. (Suitably stylized, this might sound familiar to Americans. The marriage of opposites that was the old Democratic Party was arguably critical to the *lack* of polarization in the US system before the 1970s. See Chapter 10.)

But this meant that when the PCs won, their coalition was radically incoherent, including francophones and francophobes, social and economic conservatives and technocrats from North America's most interventionist jurisdiction. The party ruled on this basis from 1984 to 1993, but in the latter year the coalition exploded. Failure to deliver on constitutional promises led key Quebec Members of Parliament (MPs) to form the Bloc Quebecois. For the first time, Quebec voters were offered a secessionist choice in a federal election, and the new party won a majority of the province's seats. In the four western provinces, the Reform Party broke through on the right flank. The breakthrough happened during the campaign and was not inevitable. The PCs were all but eliminated from Parliament but continued to divide the overall right-wing vote. The system stretched rightward, but the center still held, as the Liberals were back in power. They were helped by the fact that the party to their left, the labor-oriented New Democratic Party (NDP), lost about half the base that it had accumulated over the previous three decades.

There followed a decade of maneuver and strategizing on the right. Reform renamed itself the Alliance, a signal that its leaders grasped the imperative to grow. They did not abandon core conservative objectives, however, and when they finally merged with the PCs, it was on Alliance's terms. The name of the new Conservative Party is unambiguous. With the right now united, the Liberal grip on power loosened and in 2006 the Conservatives took power. They began with a feeble plurality but strengthened it in 2008 and secured an outright majority in 2011.

Over this same period, the NDP recovered, in effect stretching the system's left flank. If on the eve of the 2011 election it still seemed a minor party, this was an artifact of the electoral system, and the 2011 election reversed the Liberal-NDP difference. The key for the NDP was a breakthrough in Quebec, which in turn induced shifts in the rest of the country.[1] The NDP's newfound competitiveness in Quebec helped make it a strategic choice elsewhere, too. The 2011 shift, like the 1993 one, has elements of accident. Accident or not, by weakening the Liberals, it enhanced polarization in Parliament.

Did this reflect shifts in the electorate? Unfortunately, there is no comprehensive indicator that goes back to the years before the fragmentation of 1993, or even before the

---

[1]Richard Johnston, "A Realigning Canadian Election?" *The Monkey Cage*, May 3, 2011. http://www.themonkeycage.org/2011/05/03/a-realigning-canadian-election/.

reconsolidation of 2004. We can, however, get some purchase on events since 2004. The 2004 Canadian Election Study (CES) included the 11-point left-right scale that is now standard in the CSES, and repeated it in 2008 and 2011.[2]

Over that span, party groups remained pretty much fixed in place ideologically, as Figure 26 shows. (In the graph, the 0-10 scale has been reset and centered for interpretive clarity.) Party identifiers are slightly more polarized than voters, not surprisingly, but within groups is there no obvious trend of increasing polarization. Similarly, the overall ideological dispersion in the sample has not grown: standard deviations of 0.38 to 0.41 depending on whether the calculation is based on the whole sample or just on voters or identifiers. Instead, the vote of the flanking parties, the Conservatives and NDP, has grown, while that of the Liberals in the center has been cut in half. So the big battalions now are on the flanks, rather than in the middle.

The exact numbers should be taken with a grain of salt, perhaps, but the basic point is that the Canadian system has polarized as a result of shifts in the menu of choices. Canadians' ideological locations are probably better sorted by party than they were 30 years ago, especially on the right. But this sorting was not ineluctable. The shifts embody a large dose of contingency, with Quebec as a major source, amplified by strategic induction through the electoral system.

---

[2]"Home," *Canadian Election Study*, accessed September 24. http://www.ces-eec.org/pagesE/home.html; "Comparative Study of Electoral Systems," *Comparative Study of Electoral Systems*, accessed September 24, 2014. http://www.cses.org/.

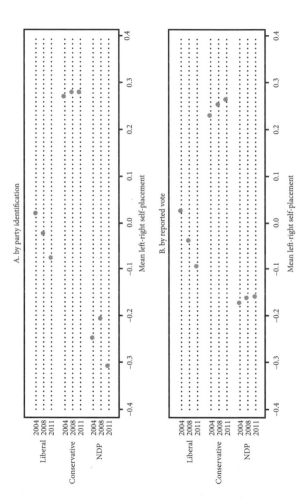

Figure 26 Polarization of Partisans—Canada 2004–11.
Data from Canadian Election Studies.

Discussion questions

- How has the Canadian party system changed and why has this resulted in polarization?
- Are the shifts in the party system visible in survey data?

Further reading

Johnston, Richard (2008), "Polarized Pluralism in the Canadian Party System," *Canadian Journal of Political Science* 41 (December): 815–34.

20

In Britain, polarization could be the solution

Robert Ford

Political polarization is hurting America. This is the message from pundits on both sides of the political divide: American politics has become angry and tribal (see Chapter 2 and 8). Rational government has become impossible, as even keeping the federal government's doors open and getting the bills paid has become a titanic struggle. If only America had parties willing to compromise with each other and stand up to the grassroots, the lament continues. Partisan voters on each side would be less tribal, policy would be more rational and responsive, and everyone would be happier. Right?

Not so fast. Across the pond here in Britain, the political trends have run in the opposite direction from those in America since the early 1990s, when the traditional governing parties in Britain—the Conservatives and Labour—elected relatively moderate leaders.[1] The British have been governed

---

[1]James Adams, Jane Green, and Caitlin Milazzo, "Has the British Public Depolarized Along with Political Elites? An American Perspective on British Public Opinion," *Comparative Politics Studies* 45, 4 (2012): 507–30.

for 20 years by pragmatic parties, focused on the center and happy to steal each other's ideas. Has this made for a contented electorate? Not at all. Turnout in British elections has slumped since this convergence began, as Figure 27 shows, leading to debate about a crisis in British democracy.[2] Between 1992 and 2001, nearly one in five British voters stopped showing up on polling day, and most have not returned. Trust in politicians and satisfaction with politics have also fallen.[3] Party identification and party member-ships have collapsed to their lowest levels in modern history.[4] Growing numbers of voters now either ignore politics entirely, or express their hostility to the mainstream

[2]Catherine Bromley, John Curtice, and Ben Seyd, *Is Britain Facing a Crisis of Democracy* (London: The Constitution Unit, 2004); Patrick Dunleavy, Chris Gilson, and David Sanders, "Is the UK Electorate Disengaged," *British Politics and Policy*, March 10, 2010. http://www.blogs.lse.ac.uk/politicsandpolicy/is-the-uk-electorate-disengaged/; "How Democratic is the UK? The 2012 Audit," *Democratic Audit UK*, accessed September 24, 2014. http://www.democraticaudituk.files.wordpress.com/2013/06/exec-summary.pdf.

[3]"Trust, Politics, and Institutions," *British Social Attitudes 30*, accessed September 24, 2014. http://www.bsa-30.natcen.ac.uk/read-the-report/key-findings/trust,-politics-and-institutions.aspx; Ben Seyd, "Why Are Citizens in Britain Discontented with Politics?," *Political Studies Association*, October 10, 2013.http://www.psa.ac.uk/insight-plus/blog/why-are-citizens-britain-discontented-politics.

[4]Harold D. Clarke, David Sanders, Marianne C. Stewart, and Paul F. Whitely, *Political Choice in Britain* (Oxford: Oxford University Press, 2004); Richard Keen and Feargal McGuinness, "Membership of UK Political Parties," *Parliament.uk*, September 23, 2014. http://www.parliament.uk/business/publications/research/briefing-papers/SN05125/membership-of-uk-political-parties; Ross Clark, "End of the Party: How British Political Leaders Ran out of Followers," *The Spectator*, September 14, 2014. http://www.spectator.co.uk/features/9019201/the-end-of-the-party/.

parties by backing the radical new entrant, the United Kingdom Independence Party (UKIP). After 20 years of rising polarization, America's voters hate their politicians. Yet, after 20 years of steady moderation, Britain's voters seem to hate their politicians too. What is going on?

Polarization leaves moderate voters without a voice in politics; centrism leaves voters at the extremes without a voice, and similarly unhappy about it, as recent research illustrates.[5] What is more, centrism may be more of a problem for parties, because political activists tend to hold more extreme views.

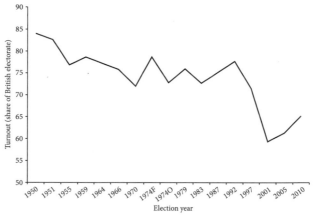

Figure 27 Declining turnout in British elections.

[5]Heinz Brandenburg and Robert Johns, "The Declining Representativeness of the British Party System, and Why it Matters," *Political Studies* 62, 4 (2013): 704–25.

Moderation may bring parties closer to the average citizen, but it also hollows them out, starving them of the activists and funders they rely on to communicate with voters. All the main British parties have seen a slump in membership and donations over the past two decades, leaving them unable to undertake even basic voter mobilization in many districts.

Political moderation can also result in deep political divisions being neglected. America's supposed golden age of deal-making moderates, the 1930s–1960s, came about in part due to the willingness of southern conservative Democrats to adopt moderate economic positions to defend segregation. As discussed in Chapter 10, current American polarization partly reflects the re-organization of southern racial and class conflicts back into politics. In Britain, the long-standing conflict is over class alone, and the recent dynamic has operated in the opposite direction. After a series of election defeats, the traditionally working-class Labour party refocused on winning the middle class, and the class conflict which had defined British politics was no longer a central source of party competition.[6] This made perfect strategic sense for Labour, and delivered three successive election victories under Tony Blair. But it came at a price. Turnout slumped, and the share of voters saying they

[6]Geoffrey Evans and James Tilley, "How Parties Shape Class Politics: Explaining the Declines of the Class Basis of Party Support," *British Journal of Political Science* 42, 1 (2012): 137–61; Geoffrey Evans and James Tilley, "The Depoliticization of Inequality and Redistribution: Explaining the Decline of Class Voting," *The Journal of Politics* 74, 4 (2012): 963–79.

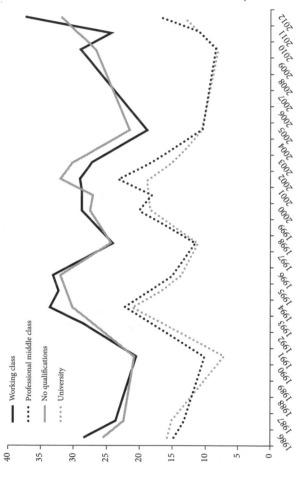

Figure 28 Share of British respondents who strongly agree that "people like me have no say in government" 1986–2012, by social group.

saw no difference between the parties shot up.[7] Such voter dissatisfaction is highest among working-class voters, as Figure 28 illustrates, and has recently risen to all-time highs in these groups, as the voters hit hardest by unemployment, declining real wages, and government austerity policies find they have no voice in mainstream politics.

Britain's combination of moderate politicians and unhappy voters is also a consequence of differences in the way British and American politics are organized. In both countries, we find a significant section of the electorate—older, white, and socially conservative—adopting a "stop the world I want to get off" attitude. These voters are unhappy with the changes of recent decades on issues like immigration, gay rights, and race, as well as more recent flashpoints like "Obamacare" in the United States and the European Union in Britain. In America, this new political movement has been organized into mainstream party conflict in the form of the Tea Party revolt within the Republican Party.[8] In Britain, where party politics is more centrally controlled, the rebels have decamped to a new party, UKIP, which has made a lot of noise but at present lacks representation in the British Parliament.[9] While in America the political establishment has no choice but to reckon with the Tea Party, which now has many supporters

---

[7]Jane Green, "Party and Voter Incentives at the Crowded Centre of British Politics," *Party Politics* (2013).

[8]Christopher S. Parker and Matt A. Barreto, *Change They Can't Believe In: The Tea Party and Reactionary Politics in America* (Princeton: Princeton University Press, 2013).

[9]Robert Ford and Matthew J. Goodwin, *Revolt on the Right: Explaining Support for the Radical Right in Britain* (London: Routledge, 2014).

in Congress, in Britain politicians are tempted to ignore the UKIP revolt, as the new party has little prospect of winning many seats. Yet ignoring a revolt backed by one voter in ten, including large swaths of Labour's traditional white working-class base, risks legitimating UKIP's core argument that the political parties ignore British voters.

The more fragmented British party system also brings a cautionary tale for those advocating the establishment of a centrist third party as a solution to America's current political polarization.[10] Britain has always had a significant centrist third party, but this prevented neither the polarization of the Thatcher era nor the more recent political convergence. What is more, voters have not rewarded Britain's centrist party, the Liberal Democrats, for exercising a moderating influence in government. The party's support has collapsed since it joined the right-wing Conservatives in a coalition government: around 60 percent of Lib Dems switched away from the party during its first year in government, and the party has had little success trying to woo centrists from the other parties.[11] They now face an electoral bloodbath.

[10]Brendan Nyhan, "The Third Party Fever Dream," *Columbia Journalism Review*, February 15, 2013. http://www.cjr.org/united_states_project/the_third_party_fever_dream.php?page=all.

[11]Rob Ford, Will Jennings, and Mark Pickup, "Polling Observatory Conference Season Update #1 – Liberal Democrats," *Ballots & Bullets*, September 20, 2013. http://www.nottspolitics.org/2013/09/20/polling-observatory-conference-season-update-1-liberal-democrats/; "Polling Observatory Conference Updates #1: Lib Dems & UKIP Battling for Third Place in 2015," University of Nottingham, September 21, 2012. http://www.blogs.nottingham.ac.uk/politics/2012/09/21/polling-observatory-conference-updates-1-lib-dems-ukip-battling-for-third-place-in-2015/.

British political moderation has brought many benefits—both governing parties are impressively pragmatic and focused on a common set of goals prized by moderate voters, such as growth, fiscal stability, and strong public services. It is quite a change from the ideological and class warfare of the Thatcher years. But this moderation has come at a cost, marginalizing those with more intense political views, and hollowing out the political parties' activist bases. The major parties' moderation has also sidelined real conflicts over economic inequality and social class without resolving them, leaving voters with the feeling that politicians are out of touch and unresponsive.

As America grapples with the problems of polarization, centrist politics, perhaps launched by a third party, looks like an enticing panacea. This is an illusion: moderation may solve some problems, but in deeply divided societies like America and Britain, it cannot be achieved without marginalizing many voters. Pushing unresolved conflicts out of the system may produce calmer politicians, but it also produces angrier voters, who may turn against the democratic system which denies them a voice. In politics, everything comes with a price. Moderation is no exception.

Discussion questions

- Why has moderation seemingly had negative consequences in Britain?
- What might be the actual advantages of polarization?

Further reading

Adams James, Jane Green, and Caitlin Milazzo (2012), "Has the British Public Depolarized Along with Political Elites? An American Perspective on British Public Opinion," *Comparative Politics Studies* 45(4): 507–30.

What can be done?

21

Our politics may be polarized, but that is nothing new

David W. Brady and Hahrie Han

A historical perspective on polarization helps us better understand both its causes and consequences. We agree that Congress is as polarized now as it ever has been, and that we are in a historically unusual period of sustained partisan competition (see Chapters 1 and 11). At the same time, looking at the data another way shows that the present period of polarization is not necessarily a historical anomaly.

Let's say we counted the number of Democrats who were more conservative than the 10th percent, 25th percent, and 50th percent most liberal Republican in the House and Senate, and the number of Republicans who were more liberal than the 10th percent, 25th percent, and 50th percent most conservative Democrat. (Here, we'll use DW-NOMINATE scores, which political scientists commonly use to measure ideology, although almost any other measure will work.) Those conservative Democrats and liberal Republicans are the ones who lie in what we call the "overlap" region—the region where members from both parties overlap with each other. In periods of higher ideological polarization, there will be fewer—or no—members in the overlap region, and more members in that region during periods of lower polarization (see Figure 29).

If we simply count the number of legislators in the overlap region in each year, what becomes evident is that the present period of polarization is akin to the polarization we had for much of the nineteenth and early twentieth century. Figures 30 and 31, taken from a previously published paper, make this point by tracking the percentage of overlapping Democrats and Republicans over time.[1]

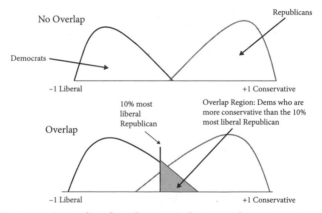

Figure 29 Examples of overlapping and non-overlapping parties.

[1]Hahrie Han and David W. Brady, "A Delayed Return to Historical Norms: Congressional Party Polarization After the Second World War," *British Journal of Political Science* 37, 3 (2007): 505–31.

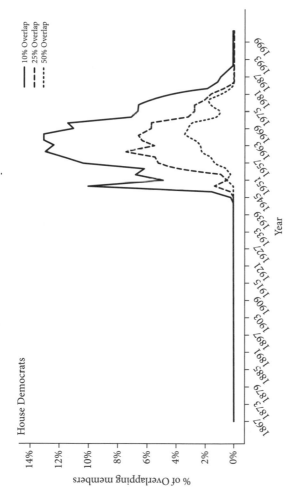

Figure 30 The percent of overlapping House Democrats.

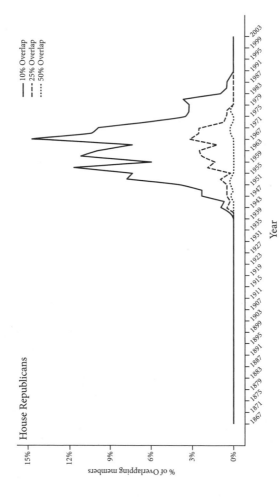

Figure 31 The percent of overlapping House Republicans.

The graph only shows the House from 1867–2003, but the story would not change if we extended it to the present Congress or looked at the Senate. Basically, there are no legislators in the overlap region until after World War II. In the post-World War II period, the number of legislators from each party in the overlap region spiked upward and persisted until the early 1970s, when the numbers began to decline. (The pattern in the Senate is remarkably similar with one exception: overlapping voting in the Senate begins in the post-World War I era at a low level, when farm coalition senators seeking support for agriculture voted across party lines.)

Obviously, part of this pattern can be explained by the fact that there were a number of very conservative Southern Democrats in Congress at the time. Yet, the historical pattern persists even if we account for that. By the 1980s, however, we are back to a flat line. There are no Democrats or Republicans in the overlap region.

These data are another way of making the same point other scholars make about the high levels of polarization we have today—but they highlight more clearly the fact that today's polarization is a return to the historic norm of polarization. From the Civil War to World War II, there was no meaningful overlap in Congress. Taking this view, we realize that it is the immediate post-World War II era that is really unusual.

What are the implications for the analysis of contemporary polarization? Looking at this data shows that congressional polarization cannot alone be the cause of our present gridlock (though, as Sarah Binder points out, they are certainly related).[2] Ideological polarization was common during a long period of American history in which our nation transitioned from an agricultural to an industrial economy and then to the modern welfare system. Even when polarized voting was the norm, government was able to achieve progress on significant economic and social issues.

So, simple claims about polarization per se being problematic or polarization itself being the explanation for Congress's inability to solve problems oversimplify the historical reality. Although many contemporary political observers decry polarization and yearn for an era of bipartisanship, the opposite was true in the immediate post-war era. During that time, which was the most bipartisan era of our nation's history, political observers wrung their hands over the inability of parties to present clear alternatives to voters. In fact, the American Political Science Association convened a task force of top political scientists in 1950 to put together a report assessing the party system of that era.[3] Their report decried the bipartisan parties of 1950, and, in fact, called for *more* polarization, arguing that more ideologically polarized parties would be more "responsible," and present clearer alternatives to voters. The grass is always greener.

---

[2]Sarah Binder, "How Political Polarization Creates Stalemate and Undermines Lawmaking," *The Monkey Cage*, January 13, 2014. http://www.washingtonpost.com/blogs/monkey-cage/wp/2014/01/13/how-political-polarization-creates-stalemate-and-undermines-lawmaking/.

[3]"APSA Responsible Parties Project, 1950-2000," *Political Organizations and Parties*, accessed September 24, 2014. http://www.apsanet.org/~pop/APSA_Report.htm.

Discussion question

- Is polarization the exception or the rule in American politics?

Further reading

Han, Hahrie and David W. Brady (2007), "A Delayed Return to Historical Norms: Congressional Party Polarization after the Second World War," *British Journal of Political Science* 37(3): 505–31.

22

Polarization in Congress has risen sharply. Where is it going next?

Christopher Hare, Keith T. Poole, and Howard Rosenthal

The most recent data show that polarization in Congress reached a new record high in 2013. Absent heightened electoral pressures or some form of partisan realignment, the trajectory of congressional polarization is unlikely to reverse course anytime soon (see Chapter 1). Members of Congress are remarkably stable in their ideological positions, and so polarization is likely quite "sticky."

Figure 32 shows the ideological distance between the parties in both chambers between 1879 and 2013 using DW-NOMINATE scores, which measure legislators' liberal-conservative positions using their roll call voting records. After a period of depolarization that ran through much of the mid-twentieth century, the parties started to become more ideologically distant beginning in the 1970s. This is true in both chambers, although polarization has progressed at a greater rate in the House. Congress is now more polarized than at any time since the end of Reconstruction.

Figure 32 Party polarization 1879–2013.

Another way to track congressional polarization is to show the distribution of Democratic and Republican legislators on the liberal-conservative dimension across multiple years. Figures 33 and 34 show the ideological makeup of the Democratic and Republican parties in the House and Senate in two Congresses: the 97th Cong. (1981–3) and the current, 113th Cong. House Democrats are shown in dotted black, while Senate Democrats are shown in black. Republicans are shown in corresponding shades of gray. The party means are marked using the dashed black/gray lines in each plot. The positions of several noteworthy members of Congress are also shown.

These graphs illustrate several important points about congressional polarization: First, the dramatic shift to the right by the Republican Party. Second, the disappearance of ideological moderates in both parties. While centrist legislators like Sen. Sam Nunn (D-Ga.) were once common, Nunn would be part of a rare species if he re-entered Congress today. Third, members of Congress who were once solid

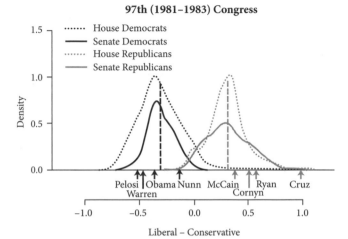

Figure 33 Political polarization in the 97th Congress.

liberals or conservatives relative to the rest of their parties have become relative moderates. We have demonstrated this point with Sen. John McCain (R-Ariz.).[1] McCain would have been to the right of the mean Republican in the House and Senate in 1981, but is today considered a moderate given the rightward drift of his party. Finally, there has been a rise of ultra-conservative Republicans in Congress. In the 97th Cong., 21 of 193 House Republicans and 11 of 54 Senate

---

[1]"Senator Robert Dole (R-KS) and Polarization in the US Senate," *Voteview Blog*, February 4, 2013. http://www.voteview.com/blog/?p=752.

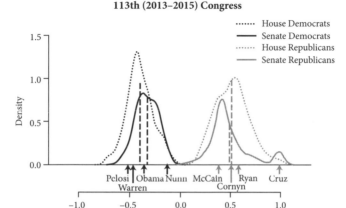

Figure 34 Political polarization in the 113th Congress.

Republicans had DW-NOMINATE scores greater than 0.5. There are now 124 of 233 Republicans in the House and 16 of 45 in the Senate greater than 0.5. Not surprisingly, this produces a much less manageable caucus.[2]

Indeed, it is noteworthy that Speaker John Boehner (R-Ohio) broke the "Hastert Rule" and pushed forward several major pieces of legislation despite opposition from a majority of his own party in the 113th Cong. (including the votes to end the government shutdown and raise the debt

[2]"The Shutdown: Boehner vs. Gingrich," *Voteview Blog*, October 14, 2013. http://www.voteview.com/blog/?p=953.

ceiling in October 2013 and February 2014).[3] These internal Republican splits reflect the increase in polarization rather than the moderation of polarization; namely, just how far the Republican Caucus stretches between the center-right to the far-right.

DW-NOMINATE scores also seem to do a good job of tapping into the rise of "partisan warfare" or "political warfare" in Congress (see Chapter 2). For example, Sens. John Cornyn (R-Texas) and Ted Cruz (R-Texas) are both very conservative legislators who vote the same way on about 90 percent of roll call votes. But it seems reasonable to characterize Sen. Cornyn as a less bombastic and more compromising figure than Sen. Cruz. Even though these differences are primarily stylistic, they do sufficiently manifest themselves in roll call voting behavior that DW-NOMINATE is able to distinguish between the two, estimating a score of about 0.5 for Sen. Cornyn and 1.0 for Sen. Cruz. There are other important nonideological dimensions—for example, a "talent" dimension—that differentiate legislators and are not explained by DW-NOMINATE scores. But polarization in Congress seems to be primarily based on ideological differences expressed in roll call voting as well as other choice behavior like campaign contribution activity.[4]

Mathematically, partisan polarization in Congress cannot continue to expand indefinitely. But there are several

---

[3]"Senate and House: Votes on Agreement to End the Government Shutdown and Raise the Debt Ceiling," *Voteview Blog*, October 17, 2013. http://www. voteview.com/blog/?p=960.

[4]Adam Bonica, "Mapping the Ideological Marketplace," *American Journal of Political Science* 58, 2 (2013): 367–86.

directions that polarization could take in the coming years. Probably most unlikely is a decline in polarization caused by a breakup of the party system (as occurred before the Civil War) sparked by some calamity like a major economic crisis. More likely would be a "cooling off" period in which one or both parties respond to electoral pressures by gradually shifting back to the ideological center, most likely via replacement (i.e., nominating more moderate candidates). Of course, polarization has been the norm in Congress throughout most of American history—it was the depolarized era in the mid-twentieth century that was the aberration—and perhaps it is more realistic to expect that congressional polarization may essentially stabilize at or near current levels for the foreseeable future (see Chapter 21). Indeed, it could even worsen if Democrats begin to mirror the Republicans' jump away from the center with the rise of unabashedly progressive politicians like New York City Mayor Bill de Blasio and the possibility of greater popular support of European-style social democratic programs.[5]

Discussion question

- Is polarization likely to increase, decrease, or stay the same—and why?

[5]Ruy Teixeira, "The Emerging Democratic Majority Turns 10," *The Atlantic*, November 9, 2012. http://www.theatlantic.com/politics/archive/2012/11/the-emerging-democratic-majority-turns-10/265005/.

Further reading

McCarty, Nolan, Keith T. Poole, and Howard Rosenthal (2009), "Does Gerrymandering Cause Polarization?" *American Journal of Political Science* 53(3): 666–80.

23

Can young voters break the cycle of polarization?

Robert Y. Shapiro

In recent years, there has been no end to the hair-pulling by political scientists and other commentators about the ideological and partisan conflict that has gripped American politics and government. Is there any way out of this mess? To answer that question, we need to look to the attitudes of young Americans, who are the voters the parties will be chasing in the years to come. If there is a way of today's political polarization, it is likely to come from how the parties—and the Republicans in particular—respond to the attitudes of young people. Here, I take a preliminary look at young adults (a.k.a. "millenials"), drawing on the Pew Center's "The Generation Gap and the 2012 Election."[1]

As is well known, 18- to 29-year-olds have been the age group most supportive of President Obama and Democrats.

[1]"The Generation Gap and the 2012 Election: Angry Silents, Disengaged Millennials," *Pew Research Center*, November 3, 2011. http://www.people-press.org/files/legacy-pdf/11-3-11%20Generations%20Release.pdf.

Their enthusiasm, however, has fallen off from its 2008 high, and they have been less engaged in politics and have voted at lower rates than other age cohorts.

On traditional bread-and-butter Democratic entitlement issues, younger voters do not stand out from other age groups. On the one hand, they seem to be more open to certain types of privatization and also give more priority to the budget deficit and to avoiding tax increases to maintain Social Security and Medicare (although their opinions may change as they approach retirement age). On the other hand, younger voters appear somewhat more supportive of government responsibility to help people in need (though such support has been declining), and have been the most supportive of health-care reform and of spending to stimulate the economy.

According to the Pew and other similar data, Democrats are most advantaged politically by their more liberal positions among younger age groups—not just the youngest—on several issues: gay rights and gay marriage; racial issues and attitudes toward interracial dating and marriage; immigration, border, and citizenship issues; as well as women in the workforce and the growing variety of family and living arrangements. The latter could be related to their being less religious. Young people are the least likely to say government has gone too far in pushing equal rights. They are also the most supportive of making marijuana legal and least supportive of the death penalty for murderers. They respond with the greatest support for environmental protection and the pursuit of alternative energy sources.

On foreign policy and national security, young people express the greatest support for multilateral engagement with allies and for diplomacy instead of reliance on military force. They are the most supportive of promoting human rights and protecting civil liberties in responding to the threat of terrorism. Consistent with these issue positions, young people are the age group most likely to describe themselves as "liberal" (although there are close to equal numbers of "conservatives"), and when asked about bigger versus smaller government overall, the age group most supportive of big government.

What has perhaps not been sufficiently recognized are the issues for which opinions of the young do not look much different from other age groups: abortion and gun control. They are also no different from others in their attitudes toward whether the Iraq and Afghanistan wars were worth fighting. They have been more optimistic regarding US policy toward Afghanistan. They have been more likely to take particular Republican positions in the cases of support for neoconservative-sounding "nation-building" in foreign policy, for a national ID card and, arguably, for free trade.

If these generational differences hold, there could well be no change in the existing pattern of partisan conflict, as long as the Republican Party can attract sufficient numbers from new cohorts through its positions on economic and entitlement issues, gun control, and abortion. Otherwise, it is poised to lose them on issues of equal rights and social values issues, immigration, the environment, and possibly foreign policy and other areas.

If, however, the Republicans shift gears on many of these issues, this could break the existing partisan divisions on them and moderate the overall partisan divide in a visible way. As we saw in Chapter 12, we can go through the same exercise for the opinions of immigrant groups—and new generations of them. Whether responding to these changing demographics is the way out of the current state of partisan conflict and its consequences—if there is any way out—is in the hands of the parties.

Discussion question

- What are the key differences in the political opinions of millennials and older generations? What do these portend for future polarization?

Further reading

Wattenberg, Martin (2011), *Is Voting for Young People?* (3rd edition). New York: Pearson.

24

How to fix our polarized politics? Strengthen political parties

Richard Pildes

The dramatic polarization of our political parties is here to stay. It is primarily a product of long-term historical and structural forces that were set into motion in the 1960s when African-Americans (and many previously excluded poor whites) began the process of becoming full political participants. That process began with the 1965 Voting Rights Act, but took decades to culminate, as it more or less now has. Thus, specific efforts to diminish polarization by one, or several, discrete changes in our electoral institutions (the design of election districts, for example) are not likely to make a significant dent (see Chapters 1 and 10). If we therefore accept polarization as a fact—as we should—our attention instead might better be centered on how to manage polarization's consequences to promote more effective governance.

My suggestion is that, if we are looking for solutions, we should re-define the problem of effective governance in our era as one of *political fragmentation* rather than one of *political polarization*. By fragmentation, I mean the external diffusion of political power away from the political parties as a whole and the internal diffusion of power away from the party leadership to individual party members and officeholders. It is political fragmentation that makes it that much more difficult, in a political world that rests on polarized parties, for party leaders nonetheless to engage in the kinds of negotiations, compromises, and pragmatic deal-making that enable government to function effectively, at least in areas of broad consensus that government must act in *some* way (budgets, debt-ceiling increases). And because of political fragmentation, party leaders in all our political institutions have less capacity to play this kind of leadership role than in many previous eras. When political fragmentation that makes it that much harder for party leaders to command their parties is added to highly polarized parties, the mix is highly toxic to the capacity of our political institutions to function effectively.

Before turning to the causes and cures of this fragmentation, here is what political fragmentation means concretely. In their first year in the Senate, and with little or no prior political career, senators today, such as Ted Cruz or Elizabeth Warren, are able to have a political stature and independent base of power that would have been utterly inconceivable in the past, even for political figures as formidable as a Lyndon Johnson. Without being beholden to, or dependent upon, the elected leaders of their parties, they can now reach large, intensely motivated audiences of potential voters and donors, in ways simply not possible before. They can establish a personal brand that stands for a different version of "the party" than that of party leaders. They have the capacity to raise vast amounts of money and act as freelance entrepreneurs, without needing any help from the political party organizations or party leaders in government.[1] This fragmentation is more visible for now on the Republican side, but that is because having a same-party president still provides significant additional pressure to maintain party discipline. But I am convinced the forces of fragmentation are just as present, if more latent for now, on the Democratic side.

As a result, the party elite—the party's leaders in the House and the Senate, and the president—no longer have as much leverage over party members (even first-year senators) as in certain past eras. This reality is part of the broader breakdown of traditional organizational "power" that Moises Naim, in *The End of Power*, so well documents across an array of public and private institutions, from churches to boardrooms.[2] The irreversible revolution in communications and technology is a major cause; these changes not only enable otherwise isolated officeholders to reach out, they also enable more dispersed factional interests to be mobilized to reach in more easily. In politics,

---

[1]Nicholas Confessore, "Fund-Raising by G.O.P. Rebels Outpaces Party Establishment," *The New York Times,* February 1, 2014. http://www.nytimes.com/2014/02/02/us/politics/rebel-conservatives-lead-way-in-gop-fund-raising.html?hp&_r=2.

[2]Moises Naim, *The End of Power: From Boardrooms to Battlefields and Churches to States, Why Being in Charge Isn't What it Used to Be* (New York: Basic Books, 2013).

these centripetal forces the communications revolution has unleashed are then further aided by the way our laws have structured the financing of elections (about which, more in a moment). As much as we tend to be drawn to stories of "weak" political leaders, it is these larger structural forces—not the failed political styles and personalities of particular individuals—that have thinned the capacity of party leaders to command.

Ironically, then, for those searching for ways to make the political process function more effectively, the problem is not best defined as parliamentary parties within a separated-powers system. That description is partly right, but wrong in an important way too. For excessive political fragmentation makes American parties today incapable of functioning as truly parliamentary ones; even with polarization, party leaders frequently cannot ensure the loyalty of members of their own party. And instead of the quixotic pursuit of institutional changes that might end polarization, we should instead look for structural changes that might restore effective leadership within the parties.

That is because political parties still remain the institutions that have the strongest incentives, through elections, to aggregate the broadest range of interests—even in (or particularly because of) an expanded sphere of democratic participation. And within "the parties," party leaders in Congress or the White House are the ones most likely to be responsive to these broader incentives—they have the strongest stakes in ensuring the broadest electoral appeal of the party brand. In addition, party leaders are best situated to make credible commitments for their organizations in political negotiations, if they can forge and force agreement within their parties. And negotiations between three to five leadership figures are easier than hydra-headed negotiations, in which new factions or individuals pop up to expand the issue dimensions at stake. Political compromise and deal-making depends all the more on effective leadership in times, likely to endure, of highly polarized political parties.

So we should use law and policy to push back against political fragmentation and to re-empower party leaders—even if this runs against the grain of American disdain for political parties and distrust of "elites," including party leaders. This process might happen organically; there are suggestions that business leaders more closely aligned with Republican Party leaders might get more actively involved in primary fights in an effort to nominate candidates more likely to adhere to leadership positions.[3] But if a need remains to orient law and policy in the directions I suggest, we might, for example, change campaign finance law to encourage more money to flow to the parties—rather than to outside groups *or* individual candidates—and to play a bigger role in their candidate's campaigns. But at this stage, specific reform proposals are less important than recognizing the role of political fragmentation in the decline of our capacity for effective governance.

[3]Jonathan Martin, " 'Super PAC' Is Formed in Mississippi to Protect 6-Term Senator in G.O.P. Primary," *The New York Times*, January 30, 2014. http://www.nytimes.com/2014/01/31/us/politics/mississippi-super-pac-aims-to-protect-6-term-senator-in-primary.html?src=rechp&_r=0.

Discussion question

- What reform does Pildes propose to lessen polarization? Why could this proposal work?

Further reading

Richard Pildes, "Why the Center Does Not Hold: The Causes of Hyperpolarized Democracy in America," Working paper.

25

Our political parties are networked, not fragmented

Seth Masket

Seemingly every day, we are told that American political parties are fragmented, divided, and weak. Many recent journalistic accounts describe the Republican Party, in particular, as "badly divided."[1] Matt Bai, at least, also sees an ideological war going on within the Democratic Party, which has, in his words, "veered back toward its more populist and pacifist instincts, venting its suspicion of the emerging

[1]Brian Resnick, "The Tea Party, Establishment Republican Divide in 7 Charts," *National Journal*, November 4, 2013. http://www.nationaljournal.com/politics/the-divide-between-tea-party-and-establishment-republicans-in-7-charts-20131104; Chuck Todd, Mark Murray, Domenico Montanaro, and Jessica Taylor, "First Thoughts: A Divided GOP Cannot Stand," *NBC News*, October 13, 2011. http://www.nbcnews.com/news/other/first-thoughts-divided-gop-cannot-stand-f8C11376124; "New CNN Poll: GOP Divided Over Tea Party Movement," *CNN*, September 15, 2011. http://www.politicalticker.blogs.cnn.com/2011/09/15/new-cnn-poll-gop-divided-over-tea-party-movement/; Emily Ekins, "The GOP Divided: Tea Party Supporters and the Republican Party," *Hit & Run Blog*, September 20, 2011.

military-digital complex, along with outright contempt for the wealthy and for conservatives generally."[2]

Richard Pildes has also argued that American political parties have become dangerously fragmented (see Chapter 24). Junior members of Congress, he wrote, were once dependent upon congressional leaders for funding and stature; now freshmen like Elizabeth Warren and Ted Cruz can just affiliate with outside groups and get that funding and stature on their own. The solution to polarization, fragmentation, and general government dysfunction is, then, to find ways to strengthen party leaders relative to their rank-and-file members, giving the leaders greater power to broker compromises and govern.

I think this characterization is not quite right. Today's Democratic and Republican parties are not so much fragmented as *networked*. Here is what that means.

It used to be pretty easy to figure out what a party was and who its members were. In the age of the classic urban party machines, local leaders like Mayor Richard Daley in Chicago or Mayor James Curley in Boston headed an identifiable and hierarchical urban organization, with lieutenants, ward bosses, and precinct captains beneath them. They managed hundreds or thousands of municipal employees who would donate their money and labor to the party in campaigns in exchange for lengthy government careers. You could

http://www.reason.com/blog/2011/09/20/the-gop-divided-tea-party-supp; Molly Ball, "No, Liberals Don't Control the Democratic Party," *The Atlantic*, February 4, 2014. http://www.theatlantic.com/politics/archive/2014/02/no-liberals-dont-control-the-democratic-party/283653/.
[2]Matt Bai, "Hillary's Question: Not If, But How," *Yahoo News*, February 6, 2014. http://www.news.yahoo.com/hillary-s-question--not-if--but-how-001804948.html.

understand who was part of the party and what their place was in it simply by reading an organizational chart.

American political parties have become much more complex in recent decades. The demise of those political machines and the rise of the civil service meant that party leaders could not just hand out public jobs to their supporters; they had to attract volunteer labor from ideological activists, which became easier as the parties moved toward the ideological extremes. Campaign finance laws prevented prominent party leaders from handing sufficient funds to their preferred candidates. Money is now raised in small amounts from a wider range of donors and coordinated across many different organizations.[3]

The modern American party is a network in this sense: It is a collection of different sorts of political actors—candidates, officeholders, activists, major donors, media figures, and others—working together to determine who gets nominated for office and thus what direction the government moves. These different actors are connected to each other in a variety of ways, including the exchange of information and the transfer of campaign money, all of which involve picking candidates and backing them at the presidential, congressional, or local level.[4]

---

[3]Seth Masket, "What to Do About Campaign Finance," *Pacific Standard*, November 18, 2013. http://www.psmag.com/navigation/politics-and-law/campaign-finance-70175/.

[4]Gregory Koger, Seth Masket, and Hans Noel, *Partisan Webs: Information Exchange and Party Networks* (Cambridge: Cambridge Press, 2009); Richard M. Skinner, Seth E. Masket, and David D. Dulio, "527 Committees and the Political Party Network," *American Political Research* 40, 1 (2012): 60–84; Marty Cohen, David Karol, Hans Noel, and John Zaller, *The Party Decides:*

The network structure makes it difficult to know just who is in charge of the party at any given point, or even who is a member of it. Is the Tea Party part of the Republican Party right now? Probably. But what about Rush Limbaugh? The Club for Growth? Megyn Kelly? Karl Rove? Any one of these individuals or groups may be influential over whom the party nominates for office, but determining the chain of command can be very challenging, especially when they battle each other for influence.[5]

Are the formal party leaders, such as congressional leaders or the chairs of the Democratic National Committee (DNC) and Republican National Committee (RNC), as powerful as they once were? Probably not, because the parties do not have the sort of top-down organizational structure that they once did. But that does not mean that the parties are weaker or fractured. It just means that their organizational decisions occur as more of a dialogue (or a debate) than a diktat.

Moreover, parties can still reach consensus very rapidly and effectively. Even in this age of networked parties, the parties organize very quickly behind candidates and are able

Presidential Nomination Before and After Reform (Chicago: University of Chicago Press, 2008); Casey B. K. Dominguez, "Does the Party Matter? Endorsements in Congressional Primaries," *Political Research Quarterly* 64, 3 (2011) 534–44; Seth Masket, *No Middle Ground: How Informal Party Organizations Control Nomination and Polarize Legislatures* (Ann Arbor: University of Michigan Press, 2009).

[5]Kenneth P. Vogel, Alexander Burns, and Tarini Parti, "Karl Rove vs. Tea Party in Big Money Fight for GOP's Future," *Politico*, February 7, 2013. http://www.politico.com/story/2013/02/rove-vs-tea-party-for-gops-future-87296.html.

to deploy a stunning array of resources to help them out in a nomination contest. Yes, a lot of fringe candidates appeared in the 2012 Republican presidential nomination cycle and made a great deal of noise in the debates, but the broader party network had converged early on for Mitt Romney, and despite the occasional bump, it was hard to see him failing to secure the nomination.[6] And this same-party network unified nearly seamlessly in the general election to support their nominee.

Now, it is entirely possible that a party network may be more prone to extremism than a party hierarchy. Ideological activists play a much larger role in the modern party system, and many candidates now come from their ranks.

Yet just because a networked party may be more extreme does not make it any less effective. What is more, trying to fix a party by running more resources through the traditional leaders is not likely to change much. Routing campaign money through the formal parties instead of outside groups, as Pildes suggests, may well help to improve the traceability of money, but it will not disempower the outsiders.[7]

Right now, groups and individuals seeking influence channel campaign donations through complex funding networks because that is the only way the law allows them to do it. If the law allowed them to donate vast sums directly to the

[6]Seth Masket, "A Newt Win Would Be Very Surprising Indeed," *Enik Rising*, December 2, 2011. http://www.enikrising.blogspot.com/2011/12/newt-win-would-be-very-surprising.html.
[7]Seth Masket, "How Do You Mend a Broken Party? Maybe with Money," *Mischiefs of Faction*, November 5, 2013. http://www.mischiefsoffaction.com/2013/11/how-do-you-mend-broken-party-maybe-with.html.

formal parties, they would do so that way. The resulting party networks might give the appearance of less fragmentation, but it is not like the groups and individuals driving polarization would be removed from the equation. In general, the network structure is highly adaptable to changes in rules, and the groups and activists that are part of the network today are not likely to surrender their influence very easily.

Discussion questions

- What does it mean to say that political parties are "networked" rather than "fragmented"?
- Why will the solution that Richard Pildes proposed not work, in Masket's view?

Further reading

Skinner, Richard M., Seth E. Masket, and David A. Dulio (2012), "527 Committees and the Political Party Network," *American Politics Research* 40(1): 60–84.

26

Gridlock is bad. The alternative is worse

Morris P. Fiorina

Frustration with the current state of American government is widespread in the electorate, the commentariat, and the academic community. Public appraisal of government in general and Congress in particular plumbs new depths. The public and the media agree that the current Congress is "the worst ever."[1] Academic commentators consider—and in some cases advocate—significant institutional reforms, even constitutional revisions.

Although I share in the general frustration, I am loath to support the large-scale institutional changes proposed by some of our colleagues. In fact, institutional changes that reduce the checks on today's governing majorities may have the paradoxical effect of moving public policy further from what a majority of voters would prefer.

---

[1]Jon Terbush, "Confirmed: This is the Worst Congress Ever," *The Week*, December 26, 2013. http://www.theweek.com/article/index/254566/confirmed-this-is-the-worst-congress-ever.

One widely discussed argument runs along the following lines. In recent decades the United States has evolved responsible parties that historically are more characteristic of parliamentary democracies. Such parties are highly cohesive and reflexively oppose any policies advocated by their opposition. While other democracies may function satisfactorily with such parties, the United States does not have the institutional structure of a parliamentary democracy. In two-party (an important caveat) parliamentary democracies such as Britain and Germany, the party that wins the most seats in the legislature automatically wins the executive (except, inconveniently, when there are a bit more than two parties, as is currently the case in both countries). In parliamentary democracies, parliamentary majorities toe the line set by the executive, and there are no powerful independent judiciaries. The majority can govern—and be held accountable.

The United States, in contrast, has checks and balances and powers shared by presidents, representatives, and senators, all of whom are independently elected (set aside the unusually powerful courts for this discussion). The system abounds with veto points that enable organized interests and intense minorities to block action. If one accepts this argument, the obvious solution is to simplify the institutional structure to drastically reduce the number of veto points and instill a common purpose in elected officials. So, abolish the filibuster. Restrict campaign finance (see Chapter 24). Make House and Senate terms the same length, and elect representatives and senators at the same time as the president.[2] Empower the presidency.[3] Unleash the majority.

But what if there is no majority? In the terminology of political science, our single member simple plurality electoral system manufactures majorities. But the fact that the winners in two-party competition get more votes or seats than the losers by no means guarantees that the winners' positions are those actually favored by a majority of the voters, only that those positions are likely to be preferred to those of the losers. Consider abortion. The 2012 Republican platform plank stated essentially: never, no exceptions. The Democratic platform plank stated the opposite: any time, for any reason. How many Americans would want a government in which either a powerful Democratic or Republican government was able to enact its abortion platform plank? Given public opinion on the issue, 75–80 percent would answer in the negative.[4] Unleashing the majority would unleash a policy with nothing approximating majority support among voters.

[2]Thomas E. Mann, *It's Even Worse Than it Looks: How the American Constitutional System Collided with the New Politics of Extremism* (New York: Basic Books, 2012).

[3]David Brooks, "Strengthen the Presidency," *The New York Times*, December 12, 2013. http://www.nytimes.com/2013/12/13/opinion/brooks-strengthen-the-presidency.html.

[4]Karlyn Bowman and Andrew Rugg, "Forty Years of Abortion Attitudes," *American Enterprise Institute*, January 22, 2013. http://www.aei.org/article/politics-and-public-opinion/polls/forty-years-of-abortion-attitudes/.

Abortion may be an extreme issue, but public opinion data suggest that on other issues as well—immigration, deficit reduction, environmental and energy issues—majorities of Americans would prefer something between the polar programs advocated by the bases of the two parties. That fact has contributed to the voter backlash observed in recent episodes of unified control of government. Roughly speaking, Democrats build their electoral coalition from the left, and Republicans from the right, but given the generally centrist distribution of public opinion (see Chapter 6), each must capture enough of the center to win. Once in office, if the party governs as its base demands, marginal members of the electoral majority defect. The result of this party overreach is the 2006 Republican "thumpin'" and the 2010 Democratic "shellacking."

American politics specialists who think longingly of responsible party government probably are remembering the textbook description of mid-twentieth century Britain, a far more homogeneous society than the United States, where political conflict took place largely across a simple economic redistribution divide. Such conditions provided a maximal opportunity for elections to produce clear majorities. Nevertheless, in my undergraduate courses decades ago, professors noted the instability of British policy (let's nationalize, no—denationalize, then nationalize again) as a reason to prefer American institutions to British. Moreover, the old thinking may well be dated. In their recent elections the winning parties in Britain and Germany failed to win a majority of seats and were forced into protracted negotiations and uncomfortable compromises before forming governments. Perversely, the result of "letting the majority rule" when clear majorities do not exist might well be the strengthening of minor parties.

As I have argued elsewhere, and as the chapters in this volume have reinforced, the current state of American government reflects an accumulation of economic and demographic developments that have created new tensions and problems and strained old political coalitions.[5] Unlike the true believers who dominate the two parties, many Americans have lost faith in the old solutions but are uncertain about what new paths to follow.

By no means am I happy with the status quo. This country faces serious problems. How long before the political system seriously addresses the problems of pensions and health care, immigration, an increasingly inefficient tax system and a variety of other problems? But failing to deal with them may be no worse than attempting to deal with them in ways that do not have anything approaching majority support in the electorate. However unsatisfying the present state of affairs, voters may prefer muddling along to ping-ponging between two minorities that attempt to govern entirely by their own lights.

Discussion question

- What might be the advantages of polarization?

---

[5]Morris P. Fiorina, "America's Missing Moderates: Hiding in Plain Sight," *The American Interest*, February 12, 2013. http://www.the-american-interest.com/articles/2013/02/12/americas-missing-moderates-hiding-in-plain-sight/.

Further reading

Fiorina, Morris P. (2013), "America's Polarized Politics: Causes and Solutions," *Perspectives on Politics* 11(3): 852–9.

Index